★ From Both Sides Now ★

From Both Sides Now

A Memoir of Transsexuality

One Woman's
Journey to Love
and Living Life
to the Fullest

★ Alexus Sheppard ★

Copyright © 2017 by Alexus Sheppard

All rights reserved. No part of this publication may be reproduced, distributed, or transmitted in any form or by any means, including photocopying, recording, digital scanning, or other electronic or mechanical methods, without the prior written permission of the publisher, except in the case of brief quotations embodied in critical reviews and certain other noncommercial uses permitted by copyright law. For permission requests, please email: alexussheppard@mac.com.

Published 2017

Printed in the United States of America
ISBN: 978-0-9982836-0-9
E-ISBN: 978-0-9982836-1-6
Library of Congress Control Number: 2016920628

Cover and interior design by Tabitha Lahr
Cover photo and many of the interior professional images of the author are included courtesy of Shirlee Robinson, owner of Leading Lady Photography in Aurora, Colorado. http://leadingladyphoto.com
Wedding photos courtesy of L&M Photography, Eureka, CA

For information, contact: alexussheppard@mac.com

The author has changed some names, places, and recognizable details to protect the privacy of friends and family members mentioned in the book.

Contents

Preface xi
A Note to My Reader xii

★ **PART ONE**
GENDER IDENTITY DYSPHORIA PHASE, 1996–1998

Trans 101 3

Chapter 1.	My "Coming Out" Story (1996–1997)	6
Chapter 2.	Regarding Photographs	13
Chapter 3.	Flying "En Femme" (1997)	15
Chapter 4.	Step on My Face, "PLEASE" (1997)	22
Chapter 5.	Going to Strip Clubs En Femme (1997)	27
Chapter 6.	Strip Clubs En Femme, Part II (1997)	34
Chapter 7.	My Spiritual Journey (Prior to GID) (1997–1998)	38
Chapter 8.	Telling the Children (1997)	50
Chapter 9.	Cancer (1998)	58
Chapter 10.	She's BACK!!! (1998)	62
Chapter 11.	Alexandra Becomes Alexus (1998)	65

★ **PART TWO**
TRANSITIONAL PHASE, 1998–2000

Chapter 12. Transsexual and Not Just CD? (1999) 71

Chapter 13. Being "Out There" (1998) 76

Chapter 14. Alexus Goes to Church (1998) 81

Chapter 15. Writings (1999) 85

Chapter 16. Erika's Story (1999) 91

Chapter 17. Thirty-Year High School Class
Reunion (2000) 98

Chapter 18. Gender Confirmation Surgery (2001) 102

★ **PART THREE**
POST-OPERATIVE LIFE, 2001–PRESENT

Chapter 19. A Retrospective on My Transition (2003) 121

Chapter 20. My Thoughts on the BBL Controversy:
Is Autogynephilia a Real Diagnosis? (2004) ... 125

Chapter 21. Stealth? (2005) 130

Chapter 22. How We Met and Our Brief
Courtship (2006) 136

Chapter 23. Our Engagement (2006–2007) 150

Chapter 24. The Wedding (2007) 165

Chapter 25. My Next Chapter in Life? (2007) 173

Chapter 26. My Evolution to Second Mom
Status (2007) 176

Chapter 27. When Did I Know? 20/20 Episode
Sparks 20/20 Hindsight (2007) 181

Chapter 28.	Living and Cruising Aboard Our Yacht (2008)	186
Chapter 29.	My TV Debut (2010)	191
Chapter 30.	The Dilemma of Hair (2014)	194
Chapter 31.	"Formerly" Transsexual? (2014)	198
Chapter 32.	The Art of "Passing" (2015)	202
Chapter 33.	Hormones (2015)	210
Chapter 34.	Nikki's Story: My Dad is a Transgender Lesbian (2016)	213
Chapter 35.	From Puberty to Senior Citizen in Only Eighteen Years (2016)	225

Epilogue. Random Spiritual Musings	231
Appendix: Cancer Blog	234
Acknowledgments	247
About the Author	249

To my wonderful wife, Deborah, my beautiful daughters, Nikki and Erika, my very dear friend Cristina and her delightful daughter, Emily. Without you, this book would have never been possible.

Preface

November 1998   July 2000

The stories in this book are the real-life description of what happens when someone tries desperately to deny their true and authentic self. As you will learn, I lived most of my life as an overachieving, perfectionistic, politically conservative, heterosexual, midwestern, All-American male. And by all external measures, I was quite successful.

Unfortunately, the angst, turmoil, and conflicted inner feelings that go along with living a lie is a condition you can only survive for so long. It's definitely not a fulfilling way to live, and in my case, the distress that accompanied living a false life nearly killed me. This is the story of an All-American boy who survived to become something quite different. These are the true revelations of a life as viewed "from both sides now."

A Note to My Reader

These two pictures were taken back in 1997 by the same photographer, about two hours apart. And yes, they are both of me. This is the first time I have ever published a pre-transition picture of myself. My legal name was Allen Tomlinson. When "en femme" I went by Alexandra Angel. Sharing all of that feels quite uncomfortable; it makes me feel exposed and vulnerable.

In fact, openly exposing my complete male history feels very much the same as it once felt to hide my desires to become feminine.

The more things change, the more they stay the same . . . I am writing this book primarily because I am a postoperative transsexual woman. I have owned and operated a transgender resource website for nearly two decades. Over the years, the large number of e-mails I have received from people from around the globe has consistently reinforced my belief that there is still a need for a book like this—one that can educate and encourage. I also feel that my experience of having lived in the world from the perspective of both genders gives me insight that is unique to the long-term, fully transitioned transsexual community. I have truly seen the world from two completely different points of view. As is the case for other things in life, perspective changes not only what you can see but also what you can comprehend. And understanding is the first step toward acceptance.

I want this book to be authentic and meaningful for my readers. As a result, I will consistently strive to move into that "feeling place" where all growth occurs. My intention for this book is that it will become a resource for GID (Gender Identity Dysphoria) education, introspection, and inspiration. I am, therefore, committed to sharing everything from my past that I feel could possibly be relevant to those who are still struggling. I also hope to provide a meaningful resource for the trans allies out there.

That said, there are already numerous clinical, medical, and psychological GID resources in print and on the web, so I am not going to directly address the standards of care regarding diagnosis and treatment in these pages. Instead, I am going to share the human side of my experience.

The last eighteen years of my life have been marked by three distinctly different phases. For the purpose of this book, I am going to call these phases the Gender Identity Dysphoria Phase, the Transitional Phase, and my Postoperative Life. I've divided this memoir into three corresponding parts, with a brief introduction at the beginning of each section.

What you are going to see in the first section is a collection of writings and photographs from 1996 to 1999. These writings come from a time when I was a gender-conflicted, married, heterosexual, sex-addicted, sometimes misogynistic, cross-dressing man living in Denver. (My current perspective is as a confident and mature lesbian woman living in the San Francisco Bay Area of Northern California.) Regardless of how dramatic my personal changes have been, that change in perspective does not alter the historical relevance of these earlier writings, or the possibility that they could be helpful to others.

The writings will be presented as separate chapters, and the years in which they were written will be indicated in the chapter title. While I have edited these writings for clarity, I've chosen to publish them essentially unchanged from their original form. This is extremely difficult for me, since my current-day perspective is so dramatically different. Now, as I reread them, I consistently feel compelled to rewrite, edit, modify, soften, feminize, or otherwise change them, as they no longer embody my current feelings. I fear that if I publish writings from nearly two decades ago, people will assume that is how I still feel. But as the saying goes, "If you quote me, date me." Please keep that in mind as you read my old writings and view the situations and settings of my old photos. In this regard, context means everything.

Though I have not changed those original writings (to avoid potentially ruining the historical relevance of my worldview at that time), I have made a few minor alterations to the text, using parentheticals to provide clarification or additional information. I have also added a section at the end of each chapter offering my current perspective on that chapter's contents.

PART ONE

Gender Identity Dysphoria Phase
(1996–1998)

Writing this book is giving me the opportunity to metaphorically go back in time. As I am rereading these old stories and looking at these old photos, I'm realizing how much I've changed.

I wrote this first story in 1997. At that time I was still very much in denial about being transsexual. I was "trying on" every form of transgender expression I could find, because nobody *wants* to be transsexual. (My own coming to terms with being transsexual came about two years after I wrote this story.) I was trying desperately to be just another cross-dressing straight man and hoped that by expressing my feminine side once or twice a week, the pervasive and ever-present dysphoria I was experiencing would subside. I was also singing live at various drag shows around Denver and performing every chance I got. I was going to fetish events and experimenting with bondage because I had a close friend who was a dominatrix. I was flying around the country and going to transgender conventions where I could live for days at a time as a woman. But needless to say, nothing stopped the gender dysphoria.

At that time, when "en femme," I went by Alexandra Angel.

I include these old stories in this book because I know there are many people reading this book who are struggling with Gender Identity Dysphoria. If just one of my stories regarding transition, personal growth, and spiritual development can be of help to those still struggling with GID, then my goal for writing this book will have been achieved.

Trans 101

A lot has changed in the transgender community since I started my journey many years ago. Much of the terminology has evolved and new words have been added. Whenever a new term will better define an outdated word or clarify a phrase more completely, I will either insert the new word or words in parentheses or describe the new terminology in the end of chapter dialogue.

Knowing that some of my readers may still be in the learning process regarding transgender issues, and knowing that this book might very well be the first book some people will read on the subject, it's important to begin with some basic definitions and differentiation between the most common forms of transgender expression. The following descriptions are broad, generalized, and open to individual interpretation from within the transgender community.

It is beyond the scope of this book to go into great detail regarding the broad spectrum of transgender expression, so I'll limit my explanation to the four most common categories. Please keep in mind that these descriptions are very basic and there is often significant overlap and crossover between the categories. You can never be certain of exactly where a person fits into the transgender spectrum without knowing them personally or speaking with them individually.

Transgender: The term "transgender" is often used as umbrella term to include anyone who crosses the traditional binary gender boundaries—hence the term "trans," from the Latin word meaning, "to cross." The transgender umbrella includes drag queens, crossdressers, transvestites, transsexuals, and people who are bi-gender or genderqueer, as well as anyone who doesn't feel as if they fit within the neat and tidy gender binary construct of Western society.

Drag Queens: Typically gay men who like to dress and perform as women. They are sometimes called "female impersonators" and they have no internal conflict regarding their gender. They often dress quite dramatically, and when it comes to gown selection, makeup, and hair, the more flamboyant, the better.

Crossdressers: Usually straight married men who like to express their feminine side by occasionally dressing as women, but here again, they usually have no internal conflict regarding their birth gender. They typically dress more conservatively than drag queens and may present as a more traditional lady of society, professional woman, or housewife. (I wanted desperately to fit into this category!) By numbers, this is probably the most represented group at popular transgender conferences and conventions.

Transvestites: Crossdressers who are primarily fetish-driven and tend to wear leather, rubber, PVC, latex, or other less traditional items of clothing. They may be interested in bondage or S&M, or other fetish forms of expression. Once again, there is usually no gender dysphoria.

Transsexuals: Those who have (or have had) severe gender dysphoria and feel as if they were "born in the wrong body" (though I really dislike that phrase). Not everyone who is transsexual will have surgery to change their body, but Gender Confirmation Surgery, formerly called sexual reassignment surgery, is an important part of the transitional process for many of us.

I'll say much more about transsexuality in the later chapters.

Chapter 1

My "Coming Out" Story
(1996–1997)

I was just about to turn forty-five when I discovered my hidden feminine self. One night in December of 1996, my wife of twenty-one years came to bed wearing a sexy teddy, garter belt, and stockings. I commented on how great she looked, to which she replied, "If you think I look so great why don't you try it on?"

Being the macho male self I was at the time, I immediately replied "NO WAY!"

My wife persisted for a minute or so, but I was unable to allow myself to even consider the thought of wearing her lingerie that night. After we made love, I pondered why she would ask me to wear her most intimate apparel, and why I was unable to comply. I figured she would not have asked if she did not want to see me in such things. So I made a mental note to surprise her by dressing in her lingerie before she came to bed the next night.

I went upstairs a few minutes early the next night so I could find just the right lingerie, garter, and stockings and still have time to put them all on as she got our two children to bed. All men who like to wear women's clothes know what I experienced next. As I slid on the first stocking, I experienced such a rush of ecstasy that it both surprised and overwhelmed me. I was immediately sexually aroused, but the feeling went much, much deeper than mere sexual arousal.

My wife came into the room while I was still dressing, and commented, "My, my, it looks like you are having fun!"—to which I replied, "You cannot know how much fun I am having." The mixture of feelings I was experiencing included joy, excitement, sexual arousal, confusion, fear, and ecstasy all at the same time. This high was better than anything I had ever experienced with drugs or alcohol. My wife commented on how great my legs looked in hose, and we had a good time making love while I wore her lingerie. As I fell asleep, I pondered the events and feelings of the evening. How could a macho guy like myself possibly enjoy wearing women's stockings?

Little did I know that Pandora's box had been opened.

The next night I decided to test these feelings again, but this time with a different piece of lingerie—and as you might guess, the result was the same. My wife was as surprised with the repeat performance as I was; we again made passionate love and went to sleep.

As someone who always likes to be in control (what an illusion that is), I decided the next night not to allow any more excursions into the realm of cross-dressing. I thought the previous two nights would be just a casual diversion into the kinky, and that I could let it go at that.

A week or so later, however, I was having lunch at home, channel surfing while eating, and I started watching Ricki Lake. She was talking about "men with secret lives"—and guess what that secret was?

The show featured three men with very normal jobs, all of whom came onstage crossdressed. I immediately recognized my feelings from the bedroom and said to myself, "I want to do that!"

I began to search on the Internet that very night. As you might imagine, there were lots and lots of links. I was pleased to find a very active transgender society right there in Denver. I found out about the Gender Identity Center (GIC), and went to a meeting that same Friday night. Of course, I went as a man, as I did not even know where to start. The "girls" there were very helpful and supportive as they listened to my story. They suggested I go to a local boutique that performed a lot of "transformations" to learn more and begin my collection of apparel.

When I first went to this "gender boutique" (a retail store catering to the cross-dressing and drag community), I was so nervous I felt as if my heart was going to explode out of my chest! I had decided not to reveal my true identity, and to be vague about where I lived. Within a matter of minutes, however, the two owners made me feel so comfortable and at ease that I not only told them my real name, I actually gave them one of my business cards. (The store was owned by a pair of very friendly gay men who had been active in the drag community for many years.) Within an hour I was the proud owner of a corset, waist cincher, breast forms, and a beautiful, conservative pageboy-style blond wig. They also gave me guidance on where to shop for dresses, shoes, and other regular items I could easily purchase at other stores that were "T" friendly, and I made an appointment for a complete makeover and photo shoot for the first Friday after the New Year. I chose Friday because it coincided with the next GIC meeting I would be able to attend. This time I would be going dressed "en femme." How exciting!

The two-week holiday break between my first GIC meeting and my first makeover were probably the longest two weeks of my life. My wife and I spent most of the holiday season with our two sets of parents, both of whom lived out of state. Needless to say, the topic of cross-dressing never came up during casual holiday conversation.

When we got back to Denver for the New Year, I had time

to go shopping for the rest of my "coming out" evening attire. My wife was supportive, and we went to Gantos at Cherry Creek Mall. There my wife tried on several dresses for me until we found one we both liked. Fortunately, we were almost the same size. If the dress was just a little big on her, it would fit me just right. (One of the joys of being relatively small for a man.) My shoe size is a woman's size 9W, so finding a conservative two-inch heel pump was easy too.

When I showed up for my makeover on January 4, 1997, I was beginning to understand that my life would never be the same again. I was so excited I could hardly sit still. After my makeup was finished I got to look in the mirror—and I must admit I was a bit shocked. I did not really know what to think, but I did like what I saw.

After the wig was on and styled, and I had on the new red and black dress, garters, hose, heels, purse, etc., I had a chance to see my feminine self in the mirror for the first time. OH MY GOD!!!!! I was truly in love! I must have stood in front of the mirror for several minutes, admiring my new self from all sides. The makeup artist then named me "Alexandra." (Since she had been active in the drag community for many years, she was quite accustomed to naming her new feminine creations.)

The makeup artist and photographer finally managed to coax me away from the mirror and we moved into their studio for my photo shoot. Needless to say, I had no clue how to pose as a woman. Here again, the boutique staff and the photographer were helpful to the extreme. (The photo that greets you at the beginning of this section is from that first night.) The rest of the shoot went marvelously, and I still had time to get to the GIC meeting for my debut.

When I showed up at the meeting as "Alexandra" after going two weeks earlier as Allen, the girls did not make the connection at first. When I refreshed their memories of our past meeting, they were all quite surprised at my appearance (for my first night out) and wanted to hear all about my makeover, photo shoot, and shopping experiences. The meeting was an absolute ball! We all went out to a cafe for a bite to eat afterward, and then on to a local bar for a drag show. I was hooked.

Alexandra was going to be quite a party girl! It was hard to believe that I'd missed out on all those years of that much fun.

MY CURRENT PERSPECTIVE

The first thing that jumps out at me regarding this story is that it was written 100 percent from the heterosexual, male perspective. This is no surprise, since I was just beginning to explore the transgender world and had barely begun to uncover my feminine identity.

The narrative mentions that I was at first uncomfortable with my wife's request to wear her lingerie. What I really should have said was that I was absolutely terrified at the thought! I had always thought that transgender people of any sort were the strangest of the strange. In fact, they repulsed me. This inner repulsion is the same feeling that causes some suppressed people to act violently toward transgender people—a reaction against those deep, dark, and completely unacceptable feelings being brought up. And yet here was my wife of twenty-one years, asking me to participate in something I considered, at that time, to be quite perverse.

Could this be because maybe at some subconscious level I already knew that the true and authentic me was about to be discovered? And was my male ego afraid that it was about to be replaced? To this day, I'm not sure of the answers to these questions, but what I confronted early on in this phase was pure fear and panic.

I said that when I first put on my wife's lingerie, I was surprised by the intensity of the emotions I experienced. That was an understatement, to say the least! It was a feeling that I can only describe as otherworldly. It was a combination of sexual arousal and a deep, self-aware feeling that screamed, "Let me out!" It was as if I was getting my first breath of air after being held under water for a very long period of time. At that point in my life, I was a conservative, professional, and career-minded man who was more concerned with status and outward appearance than almost anything else. There could be no room for something as kinky as this!

Fast-forward to actually starting to cross-dress. Not only was I afraid of my feelings from the first night of wearing the lingerie, after the second night of cross-dressing produced the same intensity of emotion as the first, I somehow knew, at a deep level, that what I was experimenting with was a force to be reckoned with. (So, in typical conservative fashion, I pushed it away with all my might!) But when the feelings re-emerged after watching the Ricki Lake episode, it became clear that the feminine expression within me was no longer going to be denied. How could I possibly be one of "them"? These feelings were completely unacceptable to me, and yet I could tell my feelings had already begun to change from fearful resistance to hesitant, albeit still terrified, curiosity.

When I discovered that the Gender Identity Center was just a few miles from my house, I was actually quite surprised; after all, I lived in the conservative western suburbs of Denver. How could such a "fringe" activity be occurring practically in my own backyard, right there in the suburbs?

I also had a mild feeling of relief, and a realization that maybe I was not alone. Apparently others had experienced these same bizarre feelings! At the same time, I was also still deeply afraid, because I realized I was starting down a path from which there would likely be no return. After all, it is impossible to un-ring a bell.

Another thing I notice in this older writing is how I refer to the other transgender women as "girls." This shows a non-acceptance of their (or my) gender expression, and is a clear indication that I was not yet aware of the broad spectrum of expressions and identities within the transgender community. It is quite apparent that my learning had just begun.

This account also demonstrates the rapidity with which I moved into my transgender expression. Once I make a decision, I move ahead with resolve and confidence—that's the kind of person I've always been. That is the primary reason I seemingly moved so quickly from being afraid of my transgender expression to at least partially embracing it. I didn't know exactly where I was going, but I did know that I absolutely must go there, in spite of my fear! It has been said that courageous people do not lack fear; it is that they acknowledge the fear and continue to move ahead. At the time, I did not consider myself courageous—far from it, in fact—but I did know I must move ahead. In retrospect, I think I can now admit that it was a courageous act.

That same willingness to try new things also contributed to my wife's support of my exploration, at least at the beginning. I was candid with her regarding the fact that I didn't know where this exploration might lead. But I also knew it was something that I absolutely needed to pursue. Fortunately, she was supportive of that need to know, though her support was reluctant.

Because of that support, at the very beginning of my transgender journey she would go shopping with me, both to try on the clothing and to give fashion advice. To this day, I am grateful for her help and support during that difficult time.

People have often asked me why my wife first asked me to try on her lingerie. That was a question I did not ask her until many months later. Her answer was quite innocent: "I just wanted you to see how uncomfortable the lingerie was!" I was dumbfounded by that answer. It's hard to believe that something so innocent ended up changing both of our lives forever.

Chapter 2

Regarding Photographs

One of the questions non-transgender people (the correct term is cisgender) ask me is, "Why is there so much emphasis on photo pages in the trans-related books and websites?" Besides the obvious societal fascination with all things "trans," the answer is multifaceted and quite individual. So I'll simply tell you what drove my early obsession with photo sessions. My photographic desires were driven by the need to see my feminine side while still living most of my life in male mode. As a result, most of my professional photo sessions occurred PRE-transition. (Once I transitioned, I no longer felt the need to have more and more pictures of myself. The third-person, feminine me was simply replaced by the first-person, authentic me.)

As I mentioned earlier in this chapter, once I got a glimpse of my authentic feminine self in the mirror, I became preoccupied with the need to recreate that visual. I have spoken to many crossdressers, transvestites, and non-transitioned transsexuals, and they've all said something similar: "If I can't LIVE as a woman, then at least let me SEE myself when I am dressed as one!" As a result, whenever I was dressed en femme, I tried to make certain a camera was readily available. Or, better yet, I would schedule a professional photo shoot and then carry my photograph albums with me (or at least have a picture or two in my wallet). As soon as I transitioned into full-time womanhood, that need no longer existed, because I could see the real, feminine me by simply looking in a mirror.

Even though I no longer personally have the need to see myself in photographs, there are many people struggling with GID who live vicariously through viewing photographs of other transgender people who have posted their pictures on the Internet. (Usually because they themselves are unable to safely express their own transgender nature.) In my early struggles, I would spend many hours on the net finding inspirational websites, because they contributed to my belief that transition was possible. I thought, *If others have done it, maybe I can too!* The websites and photographs of other transsexual women who were either in transition or living full-time post-transition gave me hope.

From time to time in this book, you will see photographs in which the faces are intentionally blurred out. This is done for the obvious reason of maintaining anonymity. I sincerely wish we lived in a society where such a request was completely unnecessary, but until then, I will respect the wishes of those who wish to remain anonymous.

I hope these photo pages (and those yet to come) will lend hope to those who are still struggling . . .

Chapter 3

Flying "En Femme"
(1997)

The picture you see of me here, flying back from Dallas en femme, has quite a story behind it. That seemingly simple act was something I would not have even considered a few days earlier. However, living en femme full-time for four days during the Texas "T" transgender convention changed a lot of my ideas about being comfortable as Alexandra.

When I flew down to Dallas with Terry and Pat, two transgender friends from Denver (their real names have been changed to protect their identities), we had a discussion about how much time we would spend en femme at the convention. Pat had decided that he would dress as a man during the day and as a woman at night. Terry and I had every intention of living the entire four days as women, and had not even packed any men's clothing other than what we were wearing on the flight down. So we firmly informed Pat that we did not expect to see "him" for the duration of the four-day stay. Pat was quite hesitant at first, as he'd never spent that much time "en femme" and wasn't as excited about the full-time venture into womanhood as Terry and I were. However, he reluctantly agreed, and the adventure began.

We arrived on Wednesday night and had scheduled our return flight to Denver on Sunday night so we could have one additional full day en femme. We all had a wonderful time for the entire stay, doing things that we would never have tried in our home city of Denver for fear of being recognized, especially in the daytime. Terry had been cross-dressing for many years, and had lived in Texas before moving to Colorado, so she acted as our mentor and guide for the entire trip. We went out during the day, every day, to restaurants, malls, nail salons, etc. Never did we feel threatened in any way. At night, we went to nice restaurants, a swinger's club, a striptease cabaret, gay clubs, straight clubs—you name it and we did it. Needless to say, we really expanded our ability to live, and act, as women in those four days. This included full-time use of our female names and of feminine pronouns.

During the four days of activities, a number of other "girls" attending the event asked me if I intended to fly back to Denver en femme. I told them no, as I thought that would be too much of a threat, even given my newly expanded definition of Alexandra. Everyone said I should do it, as they said "passing" wouldn't even be a consideration. I accepted such remarks as compliments, but didn't take them seriously.

Our plans for Sunday were to get dressed for a full day

en femme, move all the luggage into one room for day storage, and come back to the room mid-afternoon to change into our men's clothes for the return flight to Denver. Sunday morning I got up, dressed as Alexandra, and went across the hall to join the other two girls, and instead found two men inside, all packed and ready to go. It turned out that Pat was extremely concerned about getting his acrylic nails removed professionally. He had managed to pry one of them off the night before, and had found it to be too time-consuming and painful to do the rest. He insisted that he could not even consider enjoying the day en femme while worrying about getting the nails removed. He also wanted to catch an earlier flight home so he could take care of some business before Monday morning.

Terry was supportive of Pat's desires, but they had "forgotten" to include me in their decision. So here I was as Alexandra, all ready for a day full of fun with my girlfriends—but finding myself in the company of two men. They both said they would love to be my escorts for the day, however, so off we went.

We dropped Pat off at a nail salon booth at the hotel, and Terry and I began to socialize with the other conference attendees who were still at the hotel. I met several previous acquaintances "in drab" (meaning in male attire), and was often VERY surprised to meet their "other side" (meaning their male side). Since I was still dressed, they all assumed I was planning to fly back en femme, and upon hearing that I was not, insisted that I "just do it." The more I heard that suggestion, the more I began to consider it. By the time Pat finally had his nails off, I had decided to remain in character and fly back as Alexandra. Terry assured me that one pretty woman accompanied by two men would be the best cover I could ever ask for in an airplane, so off to the airport we went.

They dropped me off at the curb with the luggage while they returned the rental car. I was standing there with a large pile of suitcases, wig boxes, clothes bags, etc., when the shuttle bus came and the porter asked me very politely, "Where are you going, ma'am?" I told him our destination, and he proceeded to load all the luggage for me. I thought to myself, *Wow, this is not only easy, it is fun, too!* I hadn't known that I would actually enjoy being treated with such chivalry.

When we checked our bags curbside, the only thing the agent was concerned with was three people and three IDs. He never looked at the pictures or compared them with our faces, only matched the names with the tickets.

We were planning to fly standby for an early flight, so we couldn't check in at the gate until closer to flight time. We decided to go get a drink to pass the time, and went to TGI Friday's for a smoothie.

After four days of being en femme, we'd gotten to be quite good at knowing when people were "looking"—trying to figure us out—but so far, nobody had so much as raised an eyebrow. Terry was right: two men and one woman was the perfect cover. We waited for a table at TGI Friday's, and then took our time with our drinks. All of this happened without so much as a second glance from the waitress or other patrons.

Our drinks finished, we headed off to the gate for the ultimate test.

We had booked our flights with "paperless" tickets, so had to show an ID to get a boarding pass. We walked up to the agent and gave him our IDs, and he began typing on the computer to get our seat assignments. After he got the three seats together, he began to give us our IDs back, carefully matching the seat number with the name and face on the ID. It took about thirty seconds for him to get TOTALLY confused. He had three men's IDs but saw two men and a woman standing in front of him. After he gave Terry and Pat their IDs, he looked at me, puzzled. I leaned toward him, and in my lowest baritone voice, said, "Smile, you're on *Candid Camera*."

He absolutely flipped out! He did not know whether to

be surprised, amused, or embarrassed, or if he should call security or what. He stuttered and stammered, not knowing how to act or respond.

After a few seconds of laughter, he insisted on calling his supervisor over—not to create any sort of problem, but rather to show her how good I looked and explain why he was so confused. (I think he simply wanted to share his amazement with his superior.) As the supervisor came over, he handed her my ID, and said, "Match that ID to the correct person." She looked at the picture and said it belonged to Pat. The agent told her she was wrong, and to try again. She looked carefully, and again insisted that the ID was Pat's. While pointing at me, the agent finally told her the ID belonged to "Her, before the change!" I just smiled and waved.

The supervisor had the same reaction of total surprise and embarrassment. She said, "My God! You're gorgeous! I wish I looked as good as you!"

I thanked her, took my ID, and off to the gate we went. (That check-in certainly wouldn't be so simple today.)

The rest of the flight went completely without incident. We had the flight attendant take our picture, and she gave no indication whatsoever of concern or confusion. If anyone on the plane had any question about Alexandra, they hid it very well. Neither Terry nor Pat saw anyone "looking" at any time. Flying en femme is something I intend to do again, at the very next opportunity.

P.S. I now have an official Colorado ID with Alexandra's picture on it. That should make life easier for the ticket agents. Fortunately, Colorado allows you to have both a driver's license and an official photo ID. So I use the ID when en femme, and the driver's license when "in drab." (After 9-11, this is probably no longer possible.)

MY CURRENT PERSPECTIVE

Since this piece was also written in 1997, my writing style hadn't changed much from what you saw in Chapter 1. It's still written from the perspective of a heterosexual, cross-dressing man, and I was still using quotes around the word "girls" as a way to differentiate transgender women from cisgender women. My transgender education process was still very much in its infancy.

When I say I was threatened by the thought of flying home en femme, what I was really threatened by was the thought of being identified by the other passengers as a man in a dress. Being seen as a transgender by someone outside the community is called "being read," and going completely unrecognized by others is called "passing." (Chapter 32 is devoted entirely to the subject of passing.) But since I was going to be enclosed in a small space for several hours with a plane full of strangers, I didn't initially think I should risk the potential discomfort of being discovered or recognized as male.

I also mentioned that I had decided to remain "in character" for the flight home. This distinctly shows that I was not yet identifying as Alexandra, even though I felt more liberated at that convention than I could have ever imagined. I continued to refer to Alexandra in the third person throughout the remainder of the story, and that pattern will continue for the next several chapters.

I distinctly remember the process of mentally moving in and out of my newly discovered feminine persona. The unhappiness that accompanied the removal of my makeup, and getting redressed as male, was terrible. The process itself felt as if I were being put back into a cage, like stepping back into a restrictive and unwanted role with someone else controlling the outcome. But it wasn't simply about the makeup or clothing. It was about expressing a piece of me that had been repressed for far too long. Freedom becomes even more important once it's been taken away.

Another repeating theme is beginning to become apparent at this point: the need for external reassurance and validation regarding my appearance. Deep down, I really wanted to be seen as a beautiful woman. Cisgender women begin to experience the societal benefits of beauty, or the lack thereof, at an early age. But for transgender women, not only being seen as female but also as beautiful somehow feeds the need for reassurance in a completely different way. I think maybe we confuse being seen as beautiful as the equivalent of being loved and accepted. And who doesn't want to be loved? So this is just the first of many writings regarding physical beauty and seeking the accolades of others.

There is one other piece of my personal puzzle that is beginning to appear here as well, and that is the relative ease with which I passed as female, even from the very beginning. This will be discussed in greater detail in my later chapter on passing, but for now, just be aware that passing was never very difficult for me. Not all transgender women are as fortunate.

Chapter 4

Step on My Face, "PLEASE"
(1997)

Over Memorial Day weekend, 1997, my wife and I joined a group of TGs (Trans Girls) for an evening of dinner and nightclub hopping. We normally don't go out on Sunday nights, but since it was a holiday weekend, we decided to go for it.

We ended up at a club called 1082 Broadway at about 11 P.M. We were unaware before arriving that Sunday night is always "gothic" night at this club. The only apparel not black is the foundation on the face, which is as white as you can get it. The idea is to look like you are dead.

Not knowing we were going to end up at a gothic club, I was wearing acid-washed blue jeans and a jean jacket with a stars and stripes pattern on the sleeves and butt. My bare midriff and red four-inch stiletto high heels only added to the look, which made me completely conspicuous. I was also in my usual long blond hair (a wig)—so to say I was feeling a little out of place would be an understatement. Amongst all the black, my light denim clothes stood out like a beacon. This effect was only amplified by my red and white stars and stripes, which glowed under the black lights.

We had not even walked the distance from the entrance to the dance floor before I was approached by a stranger who said, very casually, "I'll pay you $20 if you'll step on my face with your high heels."

I thought he was kidding and replied, "Ooh, that would really hurt."

He answered, "I know, and I LIKE that!"

I still couldn't imagine that he was serious, so I played along. I asked him just exactly where he wanted to go for this activity, and he led me to the back corner of the room. There was water that spilled on the floor, and he was about to lie down in it when I suggested that he lie on a nearby bench instead. He promptly laid down on his back and asked me to place my foot with the toe over his forehead, and the heel just above his mouth, on top of his lip. I timidly placed my foot on his face, and he immediately insisted that I push "hard" on the heel so that it was pressing into his lip. I began to apply what I considered to be a lot of weight, when he reached up with his hands and pulled even harder on my foot. He said, "Push harder," and began to move his head back and forth, up and down, side to side, in a manner that showed he was obviously enjoying it.

After a few minutes of this, he asked me to switch feet so the other foot would be positioned with the toe over his chin and neck and the heel in the center of his forehead. Again he insisted that I push with a great deal of pressure, while he writhed in ecstasy. He soon asked me if I would be willing to continue this activity for another ten to fifteen minutes. I declined and said I had to get back to my friends. I did not take his $20 and went out to the dance floor to join my wife and friends. They wondered what had happened to me, and were quite surprised when I explained the story to them.

As the evening went on, I could see the same guy watching us. About an hour later, he again approached and said he would pay me $50 if Terry and I would both step on his face at the same time. By now, this was entirely too weird for me, so I quickly declined. He then went over to Terry to see if he could work out a deal with her, but she declined as well.

After we left the club, we all had a good laugh at the events of the evening. We were equally amazed that someone could "get off" by having someone step on his face with stiletto heels. It truly does point out that it takes all kinds to make a world. Compared with most of what we saw that night, we felt like we were some of the more "normal" people at the club. What an eye-opener!

MY CURRENT PERSPECTIVE
These older writings continue to amaze and embarrass me. It's no wonder that throughout the nearly twenty years of maintaining my website, I've removed these stories more than once. But every time I've done so, I've heard from my readers that I'm destroying the historic relevance of the website. So for better or worse, the writings still exist.

My differentiation between cisgender women and transgender women is still quite apparent here. Not only is there a distinction, but in referring to the other trans women as "TGs," I minimize and objectify them, even though we often used that term within our own group. The term transgender is an adjective. Anytime an adjective is used as a noun, it dehumanizes the person to which the label is being applied. They're no longer a person but rather a transgender object. Needless to say, in objectifying the other trans women, I was separating and objectifying myself as well.

I think the act of objectifying transgender women was probably a defense mechanism for me; it served to keep the cross-dressing at arms' length. That way I could speak about Alexandra and the other transgender women as *them* rather than personalize the activity and own it as a part of my *self*. I was still very much in denial of my authentic feminine being.

There was, and still is, a great deal of trans misogyny within the trans and LGBT communities. An entire book could be written about the complex social, societal, and psychological reasons for this self-loathing, but in short, this belief often comes from the buy-in that there's something inherently wrong with being transgender. To this day, popular prime time television shows and Hollywood movies continue to make jokes about transgender people and cast us as out-of-the-norm *freaks* of one kind or another. It's no wonder there is so much denial within the community itself. No one *wants* to be transgender!

The descriptions of the person who approached me, as well as the other people in the club, demonstrate a great deal of judgment regarding what I then thought of as acceptable and "normal" (whatever that is). My judgment of that guy and all the people in the club was a case of someone continuing to throw rocks from the safety of their own glass house.

I now know that it takes all types of people to contribute to a fully functional society. By definition, this must necessarily include all those who are labeled by the mainstream as outcasts, misfits, and the radical fringe. Otherwise the term "normal" could not exist. Normal as compared to what?

Now, as a member of more than one group that exists outside the middle standard deviation of the societal bell curve, I can say with authority that living as a self-identified authentic person will almost always cause you to be categorized as "abnormal" by those who are afraid of their own true self-expression. But that does not mean we are anything other than normal. And neither were any of the other people in the nightclub that night. Being a part of the societal subculture, regardless of whether that subculture is driven by fetish, sexual orientation, or gender expression, is all a necessary part of society as a whole. We cannot judge another's path as more or less authentic than ours.

Chapter 5

Going to Strip Clubs En Femme

(1997)

I must admit, when someone first suggested going to a strip club, en femme, I was quite taken aback and not really interested. The idea first came up in Dallas during the Texas "T" Party (Transgender Convention) in March of '97. One of the GG (Genetic Girl or Genuine Girl) receptionists at the Holiday Inn, where we were staying, suggested it. It seemed that she used to dance at one of the clubs, and had absolutely LOVED it when TGs (Trans Girls) had come in to watch. She informed us that not only would we be welcome, we would be accepted with open arms by the dancers. We decided that with a recommendation like that, we couldn't resist giving it a try.

We did some asking around to find the most exclusive "gentlemen's club" in Dallas, and ended up at the Cabaret Royale. The club was elegantly adorned and had several stages, and of course a very large group of very pretty dancers.

We were all very nervous when we first walked into the club. There was a group of six of us, all in formals or beaded gowns since we'd come from a formal event at the convention. Needless to say, we did NOT blend in as we walked into the main hall of the club. If you have seen the old E.F. Hutton commercial that said, "When E.F. Hutton talks, people listen," you know exactly what happened when we walked into the room: with the exception of the music for the dancers, the entire room fell silent, and EVERYONE looked our way.

The management seemed to notice the disruption, and quickly offered us a round of drinks to calm our nerves and make us feel welcome. We were then escorted to a group of tables in the middle of the club. One of our group, Terry, was approached by another customer in the club and asked if she would perform a table dance for their bachelor party. This simple request quickly alleviated our pre-entry fears about being shunned or potentially being in physical danger.

The receptionist at the hotel was right. The dancers immediately began to come to our table to dance, but even more impressive was the fact that when they were between songs or taking a break, they came over to talk to us and find out about the whole transgender scene. As is usually the case, they were all quite surprised to find out that we weren't gay, and were quite willing to talk about where they got all their great shoes, dresses, and costumes. We spent the entire evening having "girl talk" with an assortment of beautiful, hard-bodied dancers.

In another corner of the club was a group of overweight,

longneck beer–drinking "Bubbas" who had taken quite an interest in us. There was a game of "Find the Crossdressers" going, as they were absolutely delighting in telling their friends, as new arrivals came in, that there was a group of six "men in dresses" in the club. We even saw one of them standing next to our table looking over and past us to find those "crossdressers." Once they were told where we were sitting, we could hear the exclamations of "No way!"—which were usually followed by one of them walking over to us and asking to see some sort of ID to "prove" our gender. We took turns walking over to their table, answering their questions, and being ambassadors for the transgender community.

My feeling is, if there aren't those of us willing to break away from the traditional gay/les "hangouts," how will the general population ever find out that we are not a bunch of "perverts"—that, by and large, we are just regular people who enjoy the same activities as everyone else?

We stayed at the club until almost closing time, and continued to be the center of patrons' interest, and of the dancers' activity when they were on break. What impressed me the most about our interaction with the dancers was the total acceptance and lack of any sexual tension between our group and theirs. It was almost as if we had been accepted as "sisters," but with an additional element of delight and fascination on their part. I was amazed at my personal reaction as well. Not only was I not aroused by the dancers' nudity, I was also able to look completely past the overt sexuality of the setting and wonder, *Where did she get those COOL shoes?* I did not expect to experience such a completely asexual reaction.

As our cabaret-frequenting group has since found out, a large percentage of exotic dancers are either lesbian or bisexual, and as a result they are offended by the typical macho, womanizing attitude of most straight men. They are usually working the clubs just to make a good living and pay the bills. So to find a group of "girls" they can talk with during the evening, is both a delight and a diversion from the "hubba, hubba" attitude they have to deal with on an almost endless basis.

As we were leaving the club, one of the dancers, who was particularly attracted to Terry, came over to say good-bye and perform for her. Terry was wearing a long-sleeved, high-necked, ankle-length velvet dress, and the dancer took this opportunity to wiggle, writhe, and rub her nude body up and down and all over Terry's dress, much like a purring cat does against your leg. I can only imagine how good it must have felt to have the feel of soft velvet against her nude body. Terry shared with us later that the dancer was also interested in a "little more," but Terry was a good girl and declined her advances. After that, we left to go back to the hotel for the night.

On our way back home for the evening, we all agreed we would be very unlikely to *ever* go to a strip club in male drab again!

MY CURRENT PERSPECTIVE
Wow! Where do I start? There is no doubt that at this point in my development I had started to differentiate from the typical heterosexual male. But I certainly did not yet have anything that even remotely resembled an authentic female perspective. To be kind to my former self, I think this was to be expected of someone who had been active in the transgender community for only a few months. Unfortunately, there isn't a transgender "switch" that can simply be flipped and thereby undo forty-five years of male life experience and socialization. Especially when most of those years were spent overcompensating to suppress anything that even hinted of femininity, even though I was completely unaware of the overcompensation at the time.

Let's start with the initial premise of a group of women deciding to going to a strip club. With the exception of the occasional bachelorette party, it is highly unlikely that a group of cisgender women would spontaneously decide to go to a strip club on an evening out on the town. (There's a reason they're called "gentlemen's clubs.") So from the very beginning of this chapter, the entire piece is biased toward the masculine, even though a former dancer at the hotel was the one who recommended we go to a club.

There is also an underlying sexual energy that is beginning to appear in these writings. That recurring energy is clear evidence of my sex addiction. (A condition of which I was not yet aware.)

Shortly after starting my transition, I began to regularly attend twelve-step meetings for my sex addiction. While doing any addiction work is difficult, it was made much easier by the fact that for the first time in my life, I was living authentically as a woman. In my particular situation, the addiction was just another distraction to keep me from addressing the real, deep-seated issue, which was that I was transsexual. Once I came to terms with that realization and started my transition, the addiction could be seen for what it was: a now-unnecessary distraction.

As is true for anyone who has successfully recovered from any sort of addiction, there are things in my past that, when discussed, bring up visceral feelings of regret and sadness. My memories of this trip to the strip club elicit those feelings. It's not that I was actually doing anything wrong by our current Western societal standards, but the mere existence of these clubs is unfortunate from a feminist and humanistic perspective. I now believe strip clubs are misogynistic and demeaning to everyone involved. So all my current thoughts on this piece are necessarily colored by my present worldview.

One prime example of my unintentional objectification of the dancers was in my description of our clothing-related girl talk with the "hard-bodied dancers." Those words are not exactly an example of feminine companionship, even though the dancers saw us as "safer" than the rest of the club clientele. Being safe does not mean being equal.

And though this may sound contradictory and oxymoronic, there is clear evidence of male privilege in our experience at the club in regard to how we were treated there. The club managers were seemingly impressed with the level of chutzpah we were showing by our coming into an arena of masculine sexual energy dressed as women. This was demonstrated by the fact that we were given the best table in the house. This sort of unearned social advantage is typical of male privilege. Had a group of well-dressed cisgender women come into the club that night, I doubt that they would have been treated with the same level of admiration.

My current thought on the "Bubbas" in the club brings up an interesting juxtaposition. It's important that I note that at the time of the event, their game of "Find the Crossdressers" did not offend us. In fact, we actually enjoyed being the center of attention. Our participation was even more cheerful because almost none of the men were able to identify us without being coached by their friends. This, along with the fact that they demanded to see our driver's licenses as proof of gender, was further validation that we were "passing." But the strangest part of this is knowing that had this situation presented itself just a few months earlier, I would have actually been one of the Bubbas and would have gladly participated in the game from the other side! This is further evidence of both my unrealized sex addiction and my repressed fascination with all things transgender.

As in the chapters preceding this one, my frequent use of quotation marks in this piece continually emphasizes the need to differentiate *us* from *them*. The "them" changes from paragraph to paragraph, but it's consistently used to infer something inauthentic or deceptive. Of course, since I was living the vast majority of my time as a man at this point, and only occasionally having the opportunity to dress and express as Alexandra, there was bound to be confusion regarding my authentic self. Especially since I was still in denial about even the remote possibility of being transsexual. I was emphatically holding fast to the idea that I was simply a crossdresser, even though from the first night of transformation at the gender boutique, at some deep level, I'd known I was transsexual. Hard and fast denial is a powerful coping mechanism!

At the time of this writing, since I was still identifying as a crossdresser, I even used the phrase "men in dresses." And even though those were the words chosen by the Bubbas, there was no defense of their word choice. I also displayed a significant amount of need for attention and external validation from the dancers and other clients. And, as in the last piece, there is once again the repeated and significant gratification that came from passing.

As for my assertion that a high percentage of exotic dancers are lesbian or bisexual—as a lesbian woman, I am now embarrassed that I ever made that statement. I have no actual evidence that an appreciable number of dancers are bisexual and lesbian. At the time I think I had met some openly bisexual women in that trade, and I made a leap in my mind that there a disproportionate number of dancers were bi and lesbian. I also think it was a reflection of my uninformed, straight male fascination with lesbians. Now that I have been a lesbian woman for nearly fifteen years, I of course have a much different perspective, and this offensive statement falls into the category of "If you quote me, date me."

The final paragraph describes the dancer who was enamored by Terry's velvet dress, and the description was fairly colorful. The overall energy and word choice of this section was yet another example of my sex-addicted male perspective.

Chapter 6

Strip Clubs En Femme, Part II
(1997)

My friends and I had such a good time at the Cabaret Royale in Dallas during the Texas T that when we were in Atlanta for the Southern Comfort Conference in October, we decided to try our luck again. We checked around for the nicest gentlemen's club in the area, and ended up at the Gold Club.

Again, the facility was nice, and the management was polite and receptive to our arrival. This time there were eight of us, however, so finding a spot on the main floor where we could all sit together proved to be quite a challenge.

Finally, the manager asked us if we would "mind" being seated on the VIP level at no additional charge. This was an area upstairs where every dance was an intimate table dance and there was usually an additional $20 per person charge for access. We of course agreed to that seating arrangement, and were escorted upstairs to a section above the main floor, and just in front of the disk jockey's booth. He immediately announced our arrival to the house and introduced us by name, one at a time. (Just in case anyone had missed our walk through the main floor.)

The reception by the dancers and wait staff was, as before, very friendly. We did, however, find out how they managed such personal attention at the VIP level: all drinks, including my club soda, were $8 apiece (in 1997 dollars). Needless to say, we did not drink heavily.

The dancers immediately "adopted" us, and at one point in time there were three dancers entertaining our group of eight girls. After their dances and during breaks, they were full of interest and the usual questions about the transgender community. Because it was such an intimate setting, and because Atlanta allowed fully nude dancing, there was plenty of opportunity to closely examine their hard-bodied, perfect, feminine anatomy. One of the pre-op TSs in our group took the opportunity to closely examine their bodies as "research" for her pending SRS. Here again, the tone was very playful and almost completely nonsexual, although one of the dancers did take a particular interest in one of the more outgoing TGs who was with us that night.

After just a few minutes of dancing, questioning, and overall fun, the dancers were opening up to us and even showing us their implant surgery scars. (Yes, it is true, all you see in a strip club is not necessarily Mother Nature.) The conversation again ended up on costuming and shoes, as the dancers had some of the greatest shoes I'd ever seen. After all, for a significant part of their workday their shoes are all they have on.

After being in the club for a while, some of us had to go to the "ladies'" room, so we asked management where they would like us to go. They told us to go downstairs to the main level, and through a door marked "Employees Only." As it turned out, this was the dressing room for the dancers. There we met some of the same dancers that had been upstairs with us only a few minutes earlier, and were again greeted with open arms. To our surprise, the restroom section was very small, and two of the four stalls did not even have doors on them. The dancers seemed quite uninhibited by our presence, and some even went so far as to converse with us while we were urinating. Once again, we had been accepted into the "sisterhood," to the point that we were standing in the middle of the most private and intimate part of the club.

We commented on how there were plenty of "real men" in the club who would absolutely kill to be in our place. After all is said and done, who were the smart ones—the regular "macho" men in the main hall, or the "guys in dresses" in the strippers' locker room? If only they knew . . .

MY CURRENT PERSPECTIVE
Other than the fact that my friends and I are obviously becoming accustomed to being seen as members of the transgender community—when we're safely out of town, at least—there really isn't much to be said about this second trip to a strip club that wouldn't simply be a repeat of my feelings on the previous chapter. But I will expand a bit on a couple of items.

There are several more examples of my former perspective as a heterosexual cross-dressing male sex addict, and frankly, those descriptions now make my skin crawl.

One of the cardinal signs of sex addiction is a lack of personal boundaries. I think our fascination with the whole bathroom scene is a demonstration of the lack of boundaries by everyone involved. So this issue really has nothing to do with being trans or cisgender. It's simply about sex addiction and the resultant lack of boundaries.

The ongoing use of words in quotation marks continues to separate our group from not only the other male clientele but the dancers as well. So at this point, I am still very much in a gender-confused place.

Chapter 7

My Spiritual Journey (Prior to GID)

(1997–1998)

I have always been a spiritual person. Many, many years ago, I heard something once said by Pierre Teilhard de Chardin, a French Jesuit priest: "We are spiritual beings having a human experience, not human beings having a spiritual experience." That immediately struck a chord with me, even though at the time I did not completely understand all that it meant. Today, however, I use it to illustrate my core beliefs for as far back as I can remember.

I grew up on a farm outside a small town in Kansas. As on all farms, there was always lots of work to do, and I remember having chores even as a small child. Daily routine was an important part of farm life, as the animals needed to be fed every day, regardless of weather or personal plans.

Part of my family's routine included going to church every Sunday. We drove to a small Methodist country church three miles from our farm every week. We always went for both Sunday school and church. I remember getting into trouble in Sunday school for asking "too many questions." It was never possible for me to accept what I was being told on blind faith, especially when I thought there were so many obvious contradictions in what was being taught. I have always had a logical, left-brained, analytic mind; any inconsistencies or contradictions are immediately and blatantly apparent to me. For me, that created a real problem as I was exposed to the teachings of a fundamentalist Christian church, and as a result I never felt "at home" in church, and actually strongly disliked going.

In a small Kansas town, there is a lot of overlap between school life, social life, and church life. As a good student, athlete, and musician, I was always busy with activities. In a small community, you have the choice of the "party" crowd, who like to smoke and drink, or the "good kids" crowd, who go to church regularly and for the most part stay out of trouble. Needless to say, I was one of the good kids. I was an honor student, lettered in sports and music all four years of high school, and was voted "Most Outstanding Graduating Senior" by my teachers. As one of the good kids, going to social activities at church was nearly a requirement. Here again, I never liked the inconsistencies of the church teachings, but since that was where my friends were, that's where I was.

I cannot tell you how many times during ceremonies, revival meetings, and other special events, I asked forgiveness and accepted Jesus Christ as my Lord and Savior. Not once during those years did that process make me feel *any* better about myself or more at peace with the contradictions of fundamental Christian teachings.

One of the most important things I have learned in my journey is that there are many ways to achieve spiritual enlightenment and happiness. All spiritual pathways lead to truth; some just take a more direct route than others. But then, some people need the lessons learned through the indirect pathway, and that is all right, too. We have all of eternity to figure it out, so why rush?

After I left home, and throughout my early adult life, I continued to go to church almost every Sunday. I always attend a Protestant Christian church of some sort, usually either Methodist or Presbyterian. Old habits die hard, even when those habits are no longer serving you.

I am a dentist by profession. In my free time I am often busy with some sort of physical or intellectual activity. I have always been an adrenaline junkie, trying almost any sport that has the potential to give me a rush. I've raced cars, flown airplanes and gliders, owned an ultralight airplane, become a master scuba diver, ridden bicycles 2,000 to 3,000 miles per summer, owned two snowmobiles, skied downhill and cross-country, run regularly, exercised compulsively, became a vegetarian, fasted, and lost thirty pounds. I have been a volunteer fireman, a city councilman, a 32nd-degree Mason, a Shriner, a barbershop quartet member, a pilot for Civil Air Patrol, a ham radio operator, and many other things. (And yet before becoming more self-aware, I often wondered why my wife complained about not having enough help in raising our two daughters.)

I have also always been an education junkie. Becoming a better dentist used to seem like an acceptable way for me to spend lots of my time, energy, and money. At one point, I was accumulating about 100 hours of continuing education per year. I thought I was doing this to serve my patients—and indirectly, I guess I was, but I was doing it mostly for myself. I became a Fellow, was elected to the board of directors, and have been president and membership chairman of one of my state dental organizations as well.

In 1986, I began making trips to a prestigious dental institute in Florida to learn the latest in dental techniques. I was running two dental offices and constantly trying to do more, better, faster. Are you beginning to see a pattern here?

What I am trying to point out is that before transitioning, I was always looking "out there" for something or someone to fill up the ever-present "hole in my soul." Without some sort of diversion, I thought, I would go crazy. What I did not know was that I already *was* crazy! Crazy in thinking that the answer was somewhere outside of me.

In 1988, a very good friend directed me to John Bradshaw's book *On the Family*. This was the first book I'd ever read that addressed a dysfunctional family system in terms that were easy to comprehend. I now realize just how good a friend he was. This began my journey toward personal recovery. But recovery from what? I was not sick. I wasn't an alcoholic; I didn't do drugs or beat my wife. My parents were teetotaler Methodists from a Kansas farm with a successful dentist for a son. What in the world could I need to recover from?

What I resisted with all my might was the realization that what I'd grown up believing was good, loving, honest, and firm discipline was, by any outside measure, child abuse. I had a really difficult time coming to terms with the term "abuse," but this in itself was part of the dysfunction, and it also fit into our religious upbringing. As the scripture says, "Spare the rod and spoil the child." The extreme spanking and kicking I was subjected to as a child always seemed quite arbitrary to me; in essence, it occurred whenever my dad was angry about almost anything that hadn't gone right in his day. He would project whatever was bothering him onto something I was doing or something I'd said, and then he would grab me by the arm, hold my arm up, and spank me in a circle until his hand hurt, at which point he would switch hands and continue spanking in the opposite direction. This would go on until both of his hands hurt, and then he would switch to kicking me in a circle. In today's terms, we would most certainly call him an abusive "rage-a-holic."

Besides the physical abuse, there was also emotional, spiritual, and psychological abuse. I essentially grew up in a POW camp. No matter what I did or how I did it, it was never quite good enough. My father's main issue was perfectionism, enforced with lots of physical discipline. I thought if I could just be good enough, work hard enough, be smart enough, get straight A's, letter in all sports, and excel in music and any other extracurricular activity I pursued that maybe the beatings would stop. Needless to say, they did not.

I had the opportunity to spend a weekend with a very spiritual senior dentist in 1994, and he summed it up perfectly when he shared an insight about his own family with me: "I grew up in a family where my very best was always just bad enough." So guess what main issue I brought with me into adulthood? Extreme perfectionism! I'm sure I'm not the first person to achieve professional success as a result of an extreme (and dysfunctional) drive toward perfectionism. Striving for excellence is one thing. Perfectionism is a whole different matter.

I didn't know all this as a young man, of course. So when, after completing several years of advanced dental education, it became apparent to me that it would take years and years of practice in the remote mountain community in Colorado where I was living to attract enough appreciative patients to have the kind of practice I wanted (there's that search for external validation again), I decided it was time for a "geographic cure." Time to move to the big city of Denver, where there would certainly be enough discriminating patients who would come to me in droves once the word got out just how good I was. So, after twelve years of living in the same small town—the town where our children had been born—I announced to my wife and children that we were going to move.

This announcement was not met with great enthusiasm. But I persisted, and within about a year I had sold my practice in the mountains, bought two practices in a suburb of Denver, sold our house in the mountains, and bought a nice house in the suburbs that cost twice as much as the one we'd sold in the mountains.

I was instantly busier. But I had gone from being almost completely out of debt to being almost a half million dollars in debt. (What price, happiness?) But the strangest thing began to happen: after a few months of telling all my new patients about all the work they needed and all the wonderful things I could do for them, the practice began to shrink!

My perfectionism would not allow me to see the real reason for this. After all, my technical skills were the best they had ever been. I thought I was doing everything right. Never mind that my new patients had enjoyed a long-term relationship with their former dentists, and I was the new kid on the block. Never mind that they didn't know me from Adam. I was still routinely presenting multi-thousand-dollar cases to them almost every day. Never mind that all they could see was how I was seemingly more interested in their money than in them as people. To be clear, I never recommended work that was unnecessary or not in the patients' best interest in the grand scheme of optimal dentistry, but after a lifetime of patch-up, maintenance dentistry, they did not yet understand the difference between optimal dentistry and the routine drill-and-fill—and I, in my perfectionism, couldn't see the missing piece of the puzzle, the piece involving relationship building. I thought that if I were just good enough technically, the relationships would follow. Is that backward or what? Wherever you go, there you are. My issues had followed me! I had been so sure that my remote rural location had been the problem, but the problem was me.

I spent several years reading books, listening to tapes, going to workshops, and attending individual and group therapy, all to discover that the rage I felt toward my parents, particularly my father, was always being matched by equal amounts of rage toward myself, my family, my patients, the world around me, and ultimately God. I spent a lot of time, energy, money, and stomach lining to discover that blaming someone else "out there" was not going to fix what hurt the most "in here." It was time for me to pick up the pieces and go on with my life. But go on to where?

The church seemed like a logical place to get the support I needed. After all, people have been turning to religion during times of crisis for centuries. But for some reason, the more I worked at being a "good Christian," the worse I felt. What in the world was going on here?

During one of my Bradshaw weekend intensive workshops, I heard the term "shame-based religion." I had heard that term before, but was still in denial that the abuse of my childhood had been perpetuated by the very church I was looking to for support. Shame-based religion basically promotes the idea that you were born a sinner (as in original sin), are still a sinner (needing weekly confession), and will die a sinner (because after all, you are only human). But, have heart, if you are good enough, pray enough, and do all the things the church says, then maybe when you die you'll go to heaven. That didn't feel too good to someone who already had the self-esteem of whale droppings on the bottom of the ocean. My God, where could I turn for real support? It would take me a while to learn that within my question was the very answer for which I was searching.

I began an earnest search for meaning in my life, so back to therapy I went. Oh, did I mention that I was still trying to deal with the guilt of even going to therapy? After all, only crazy people went to therapists, not successful dentists like me. I later learned that all addictive personalities have a condition in common called "terminal uniqueness." That terminal uniqueness meant, at least in my own mind, that my circumstance must be SO unique that nobody else could possibly comprehend the complexity of my exact situation. So how in the world could therapy help?

It was during the next phase of my recovery that the name "Mile Hi Church of Religious Science" kept coming up from different sources. I was, at this point, more than just a little turned off by religion, and the name Religious Science sounded like a true oxymoron, so I resisted looking into it for quite a while. But since the Universe is even more persistent than I am, and since the Divine plan is almost always completely invisible in the moment, I finally relented and went to this weird, new age church.

I attended my first Religious Science service half-expecting to smell incense and hear chanting—but wow, what an experience! Before it had even ended, I could sense that my life was never going to be the same.

One of my favorite books throughout my adult life thus far was *As a Man Thinketh*, by James Allen. I had read it twice, and it spoke to me deeply. And if ever there was a religion that taught the exact philosophy expounded in that book, Religious Science would be it. It addressed that same inner sense of reality. What a relief! I discovered that I wasn't crazy after all. I just danced to the beat of a different drummer.

So what in the world does all this talk of church and religion have to do with being transgender? Everything! Being transgender is about getting in touch with your feminine side. (Or masculine side for female to male transgender people) It's about wholeness and unity. It's about learning to love a part of yourself that society says is unacceptable. It's about complete and unconditional love. If I do not love myself, I cannot love you.

After going to this new church a few times and beginning to practice some of the concepts being taught, I truly began to feel different inside. For the first time I was able to listen to a sermon without being asked to accept everything hook, line, and sinker and leave my logical, analytical brain on the front doorstep. For the first time I could question what was being said without being told I was a sinner for doing so. In fact, questions were actually encouraged. What a concept!

I decided to start taking some classes in Science of Mind through Mile-Hi Church. As I learned and studied more, the need for judgment of myself and others began to lessen. I actually became friends with a lady in one of my classes who was a lesbian. I had never even knowingly conversed with a gay person, let alone become a friend to one, before then. As an acting homophobe for almost forty years, this was quite a change for me. But the more I learned about spirituality, the more accepting of others I became. And the more accepting of others I became, the more accepting of myself I became as well. See the door beginning to open for Alexus here?

* * *

In 1996, about two years after I started attending Mile-Hi Church, I went to a three-day workshop taught by Deepak Chopra. The most important thing I learned during those three days was that if you have a desire, you must fulfill it. Desire is your inner voice, your inner divinity, telling you there is an experience you need to have in order to learn your next lesson in life. Not acting on your desires only delays the lesson, because they will return if not acted on. The sooner you act on the desire, the sooner growth can occur.

This was quite a revelation for me. I had always thought it was up to me to filter my desires and only act on the "good" ones. As desires are always messages from your inner guidance, listening and acting on them is always for the better. As long as you pay attention, you cannot *not* learn from action.

* * *

After I became aware of my extreme desire to express my feminine side, the rest moved quickly. As in all spiritual desires, movement is fast and easy once you allow things to happen. After spending about two months being Alexus part-time (which I did about two years after my first cross-dressing experience), I worked up the courage to tell my twenty-eight fellow Mile-Hi Church Professional Studies students and teachers about Alexus. Then, as my final class project—the culmination of four years of study of Science of Mind—Alexus not only attended the class in complete dress, she sang the Barbra Streisand song "Don't Rain on My Parade." The performance was amazingly well received; I have never felt so much love and complete acceptance from a group of people in my entire life. It was wonderful!

Once we can get past any personal judgments and simply express unconditional love, we are truly doing what Jesus came to teach us. That is what Religious Science, and Science of Mind, is all about. If all of humanity could just act on that one lesson, the world would truly be a wonderful place for all. (Religious Science teaches that Jesus was the great example, not the great exception. So while it is technically a Christian church, it isn't based on original sin like most Christian churches.)

MY CURRENT PERSPECTIVE

The only repeating theme I can see in this writing is the continual use of third person when referring to my feminine persona. I originally began writing this piece in 1997, when I was still going by the name Alexandra, but I modified and extended it after deciding on the name Alexus, which happened sometime in late 1998. But since I was still living almost completely in male mode, it was simply easier to refer to "her" in third person. This was especially true since my early cross-dressing felt more like a hobby than an identity (denial). By the time I started going by Alexus, however, my feminine self had begun to really internalize.

The descriptions in this writing also significantly compress the timeline from my early childhood experiences to my early transgender experiences in 1997. Most of the experiences I describe here regarding Mile-Hi Church occurred in a four-year period prior to my transgender discovery. But that period of spiritual growth was absolutely essential to my eventual opening to authenticity.

The section where I describe meeting a lesbian for the first time is actually humorous to me now. This is another clear example of how strongly we push away anything that brings up our repressed identity. A good friend of mine often says, "If it's an issue, then it's an issue!"—meaning that if you have a vested interest in pushing something away, then there's almost certainly a significant part of your repressed self that embodies that exact characteristic. This is why it has been shown repeatedly that extreme homophobes almost universally harbor latent homosexual tendencies themselves. Someone without those tendencies might disagree with others, but they wouldn't have a visceral aversion to them.

This piece also makes reference to my nearly unilateral decision to move from our mountain home of twelve years to the Denver suburbs. I didn't really consider the huge effect that the move would have on my wife and children. That way of thinking is representative of a particularly male paradigm.

I also wrote here about being transgender from only the male-to-female perspective. At that early point in my transition, I didn't even know anyone who had transitioned from female to male. So the singular perspective seems, once again, narrow and masculine.

Compared to the earlier chapters, this was a much easier writing to evaluate from my current point of view. I still remain a spiritual person, although I no longer attend church. After leaving the Church of Religious Science (for completely political and non-spiritual reasons) I attended several other metaphysical churches and educated myself about the teachings and ceremonial rituals of several other religions. I then gravitated toward Wicca and practiced that craft for two years. But once again, there was too much ritual and structure for my liking. So I stopped attending organized religious services completely.

I now believe that I am closer to my Ultimate Source when I am alone with someone I love, or in the quiet solitude of nature. I no longer need a physical structure of any kind, nor do I need the guidance of someone that has been officially "ordained" by a school or deemed a guru by someone else. My Source comes from within, and it always leads me in the direction of where I need expansion in my life.

Chapter 8

Telling the Children
(1997)

Step One: Telling Nikki

One of the toughest decisions for many transgender people is deciding when, or if, to tell their children. This can be complicated by many factors, including the age of the child, whether or not the child is living in the same home with the TG, the wishes and/or feelings of the child's other parent, whether the TG is still married or is divorced and has sole or joint custody, and more.

In 1997, my wife and I had been married for twenty-two years; our two daughters were seventeen and twelve. Both of our children were very mature for their age and good students, and they stayed out of trouble for the most part. Honesty and integrity are very important to me, so I knew very soon after the discovery of my feminine side that I wanted to tell the girls as quickly as possible. I had spent years studying the dynamics of the family system, especially dysfunctional ones like the one I grew up in, by that point, so I was aware that there really are no secrets in the family unit. There may be things that are unspoken and/or misunderstood, but there are very few true secrets. I did not want to make the issue of being transgender even more complicated than it already was by adding what I considered to be the unnecessary element of secrecy. Secrecy is usually translated into shame when present in a family, and I didn't want to feel shame surrounding my new identity.

My wife and I had quite opposite viewpoints about whether or not the children should be told. She was of the opinion that we should not tell them until they needed to know. We agreed very soon after Alexus came into the picture that I would not unilaterally make the decision to tell them, and though we discussed the subject on several occasions in the months that followed, she remained steadfast in her desire to keep Alexus's existence secret—at least for the time being.

During the summer of 1997, our youngest daughter spent a great deal of time in Kansas visiting her grandparents and enjoying farm life. During that time, Alexus was enjoying her freedom at every opportunity, as our oldest daughter, who had a teenager's busy schedule, was frequently out of the house. There were a couple of "close calls" during this time, and each time my wife and I revisited whether or not it was the correct time to tell the girls. Each time, we ultimately decided that it wasn't.

That summer, I was also in the process of starting Aesthetic Illusions, a cross-dressing service that offered complete transgender transformations. This included shopping, makeup, and hair styling, as well as an elegant evening out to a nice restaurant and later to a nightclub. With all this activity, figuring out how and where to dress outside of my own home was becoming very inconvenient. My wife frequently came along when Alexus went out, so we usually took two cars to allow me to dress first at a friend's house, and then meet somewhere "safe."

Me being transgender created a great deal of stress in our marriage, and we had numerous heated discussions concerning Alexus. And as I said earlier, since there are no secrets in family units, the children were very much aware that something was up. They did not know what it was, but they sensed something. Knowing that a child's imagination will come up with things much worse than reality, we finally decided to tell our oldest daughter.

We decided to tell her together so she would have the chance to ask questions of both of us. I began the conversation with a more general discussion about honesty and integrity. This continued into the arena of the necessity of feeling safe while discussing everything and anything within the confines of the family unit. None of these items were new to her, as we have always been a very open, honest family, but within this context, they had new meaning and impact.

I then moved into talking about performing arts. My daughter was very interested in acting and singing, and had been in high school plays and musicals. She understood how it felt to have an alter ego while on stage. Since I had been singing in a men's quartet for many years, I used this as an introduction, and then explained Alexandra as another way I "performed." I showed my daughter a couple of pictures of Alexandra singing in drag, and waited for her response.

Needless to say, her reaction was one of total surprise. She asked a couple of quick questions, such as, "Are these pictures really you?" and "How long have you been doing this?" She then quickly added, "Wow, I am really relieved. I thought this was going to be something bad." She thought that we were going to tell her we were getting a divorce, or that I was having an affair with another woman.

You could have knocked my wife and I off our chairs with a feather. We were beyond relieved that the news had been so quickly and easily accepted.

In order to stay in integrity, I went on to say that I also enjoyed being Alexus at times when I was not singing. This included a brief discussion of cross-dressing, transvestism, transsexuality, and homosexuality. She wanted to know why I like to wear women's clothes, and seemed quite able to hear the explanation. She then volunteered her observation that women "cross-dress" all the time. Children are so inherently intelligent and observant; they constantly amaze me.

We spent a few more minutes with questions and answers, and my wife talked about how difficult this had been for her and our marriage. We discussed how important communication is within a marriage, and explained why we had not told her sooner.

I showed her a few more pictures of Alexus in various styles of dress, to which her reaction was, "You're really pretty." I asked her if she would like to meet Alexus in person some time, and she quickly said, "Sure!"

As we were ending this monumental conversation, my daughter said, "I think it's *cool* having parents that aren't too straight!"

MY CURRENT PERSPECTIVE
In the first paragraph, I repeatedly use the acronym TG as a noun. As I have previously mentioned, the term transgender is an adjective. Any time an adjective is used to replace a noun, it dehumanizes the person to whom it is being applied. My early misuse was a matter of being not only uninformed but not yet ready to completely internalize my feminine persona.

I also mention the business I started during that time with a transgender friend, Aesthetic Illusions. Even the name implies that there was something inauthentic or deceptive in what we were doing. Creating an "illusion" is certainly not the same as coaching someone to express their authentic feminine identity. Aesthetic Illusions remained in business for about two years, but ultimately was doomed to fail.

This piece was also written during a time when my then-wife would attempt to be supportive by going along for the evenings out on the town. She really did make a valiant attempt, but she simply couldn't get past the realization that this new woman was not the man she married. And since I had shared with her that I thought this new persona might be the "real" me, I think she feared at a deep level that this might be the beginning of the end for our marriage.

She also really hated it when people assumed she was also a transgender woman, since she was often the only cisgender woman in the group when we went out. My cisgender wife was frequently assumed to be transgender by association when she was with a group of us, and she didn't like being the target of such an assumption.

★ ★ ★

Step Two: Telling Erika, 1997
We had such a good experience telling our seventeen-year-old about Alexus that I wanted to tell our twelve-year-old as soon as she returned from her summer trip to her grandparents. But my wife strongly disagreed. Her main concern about Erika was whether or not she could understand that this was information she could not share with her friends. Knowing how cruel children can sometimes be to each other, I understood her concern. We were not really afraid that our daughter would not be able to handle the news, but we did not want her to be hurt by her friends if she was to let the information casually slip to one of her playmates. With this in mind, we decided to wait until she was a little older.

The problem with this scenario was that she was now the only person in the family unit who didn't know our family secret. And as a result, she, like anyone in her position, was filling in the gaps in her knowledge by using her own imagination. Knowing this would be the case, we were watching our youngest closely for signs that she was being unfairly stressed by not knowing what was causing the occasional friction between the two of us.

After about a month of Erika being home, my wife and I were having another in-depth conversation about Alexus when she happened into the room. We immediately stopped talking, told her we were having an adult conversation, and asked her to leave the room. She left and returned to her own room, but we could hear her crying. My wife went into her room to console her, and I went upstairs to our bedroom, hoping my wife and I would continue our conversation in a few minutes.

My wife soon came upstairs and said, "We need to tell her the truth. She is afraid that we are going to get a divorce."

I was a bit nervous, as I had not had the opportunity to pre-plan what I was about to say, but I just trusted my instincts, and we went downstairs to tell Erika all about Alexus.

I started the conversation by first saying, "We want you to know that we are not planning to get a divorce."

She seemed to relax immediately.

My wife had expressed that she preferred I take the lead on this conversation, so I began much like I had with our older daughter, discussing my occasional singing en femme. When I showed her the first pictures, she paused and said, "Whoa, this is *way* too weird to see my dad dressed this way!" Not exactly the response I had hoped for. I waited for a few moments for her to recover from the initial shock, and then asked her if she wanted me to continue. She said yes, so I went on to tell her about cross-dressing, transvestism, transsexuality, and so on.

I must say, this was a pretty heavy conversation for a twelve-year-old, but she seemed to be handling it well, so I again paused for questions, and to show her more pictures.

She took her time looking through some of the pictures, and wanted to know more about where I went, what I did, and who I spent time with when dressing. I answered her questions, and then went into the difference between having family matters as "private" as opposed to "secret." I used the example of a young girl starting her monthly period as something that is private within the family but is not something to be ashamed of, or to be thought of as a "secret." Of course, she could relate to this example very well, and quickly added, "There is *no way* I would ever tell my friends about this."

I then asked her if she wanted to meet Alexus in person sometime, and her immediate reply was, "No way! I don't even want to be in the house when you're getting ready to go out." Again, not exactly the response I wanted, but I told her I would respect her wishes. I asked her if she had any more questions, and she replied, "No." The coming-out conversation about Alexus was finally over, though I did add that when she was ready to meet Alexus in person, she could simply let me know.

Even though I was slightly disappointed in Erika's less-than-overwhelming acceptance, I was still quite relieved that Alexus was finally out of the closet, at least as far as immediate family was concerned.

This conversation took place on a Tuesday, and Alexus's next chance to go out was the following Friday night. We made arrangements for my wife to take Erika out shopping while I was getting dressed, and for me to be out of the house by 8:30 P.M. That seemed like an easy schedule, so I was getting ready at a leisurely pace when I heard my wife and daughter return. It was only about 8:10. I shouted down for my wife to come upstairs, in case I had misunderstood. She came upstairs and informed me that our daughter had already had a change of heart and told her she didn't care whether she met Alexus or not.

When it was time to leave, I went downstairs and announced that I was leaving—and around the corner came Erika. When she saw me she quickly stopped in her tracks, her eyes wide open, and said, "Whoa, you scared me, I didn't know who you were." She checked me out for a few seconds, then walked up to me and said, "Wow, you're really tall for a woman!" She then gave me a big hug and said I looked pretty, and Alexus was off for the evening.

MY CURRENT PERSPECTIVE
The use of third-person perspective continues. This would continue to be the case until much later, when I finally came to terms with my true identity.

There is also a consistent use of the name Alexus in this chapter, even though I was still performing onstage as Alexandra and only going by Alexus when not doing drag. I think the separation of Alexandra the drag performer from Alexus the woman who went out in "normal" public areas was the early beginning of acceptance of my feminine nature. I realize I was still in denial about being transsexual, but I could at least separate my "stage presence" from my cross-dressing self. I wanted a name that felt like "me." Chapter 11 will give more details about the name change from Alexandra to Alexus.

Chapter 9

Cancer
(1998)

When I first wrote this chapter back in 1998, it was a detailed, appointment-by-appointment description of what treatments I underwent and how I experienced them. Others who are either currently experiencing cancer treatment or have been recently treated have told me the detailed descriptions are helpful and even uplifting. But for the purposes of this book, the description of my cancer experience will be described from my current-day perspective. For those who want all the detail, the entire original post is printed in the appendix at the end of this book.

On January 9, 1998, I had a needle biopsy done on a suspicious lump in my neck. They did not like the look of the cells from that test, so on January 13 they removed the entire lymph node. By the end of that week they had a preliminary diagnosis of Hodgkin's lymphoma (a form of cancer of the lymph nodes). The final diagnosis was soon completed and the result was, indeed, stage 3 Hodgkin's lymphoma. I started chemotherapy on February 6, 1998.

Hearing the words "You have cancer" is a life-changing experience. There are no words to describe the impact. It is a combination of shock, terror, bewilderment, and is completely overwhelming. It is an experience that I wouldn't wish on my worst enemy. At the same time, however, being diagnosed with cancer is both the worst and best thing that ever happened to me.

I say it was the best experience of my life simply because it gave me a clarity that can only come from a near-death experience or diagnosis with a potentially terminal disease. It gave me a nearly instantaneous, visceral gauge to measure what is truly important in this life and what is ultimately trivial. It taught me not to dwell on those daily details that are ultimately not all that important. A wise person once told me that there are two rules to live by: 1) "Don't sweat the small stuff," and 2) "It's *all* small stuff." Surviving cancer definitely puts this all in perspective.

After my diagnosis, there were only a few brief episodes, primarily in the first two or three months, when I was struck with periods of overwhelming, sheer panic. Those moments would occur at seemingly random times; they didn't have any discernible pattern. But as quickly as they came, they subsided, being replaced by a warm and comfortable knowing that I was going to survive.

This knowing came from a lifelong personal connection to my Source, as well as an awareness that the survival rate for my particular type of cancer was 60–80 percent. Not that many years ago, Hodgkin's was an incurable cancer and was therefore a terminal diagnosis. Fortunately, that has changed significantly in the past few decades.

As I mentioned in an earlier chapter, I've always been a spiritual person. And throughout my entire cancer experience, that connection to my Source never left me. As a result, I spent a significant amount of time throughout my entire course of treatment doing meditation, hypnosis, pre- and post-treatment massage, and Reiki. I even had some of the chemotherapy administered while my hypnotherapist accompanied me to the appointment and kept me in a healing trance state. I believe these alternative treatments minimized the chemo's side effects and may have ultimately improved my recovery.

My oncologist, though trained in traditional Western medicine, was very supportive of the additional therapies I sought out. They even had a private room where alternative therapies could be administered concurrently with the chemotherapy drugs. I think this progressive, open-minded approach is laudable and should be the norm rather than the exception. Hopefully this trend will expand to other areas and not be confined to a single private office in the western suburbs of Denver.

I continued to practice dentistry, albeit at a significantly reduced schedule, throughout the entire six months of my chemotherapy and part of the way through my month of radiation. When my patients would ask me how I could stay so upbeat while going through such a terrible diagnosis and course of treatment, I would tell them, "I believe that every cloud has a silver lining, and since this experience is so bad, whatever is on the other side simply must be wonderful!" Little did I know just how wonderful that other side would ultimately be.

All throughout my treatment—during times of meditation, massage, and in other peaceful moments—I was repeatedly aware that my disease had not come to kill me; rather, it had come to teach me. The old saying "Whatever doesn't kill me simply makes me stronger" felt quite pertinent, and resonated to the very core of my being.

* * *

About two months after my treatments were complete—after chemotherapy, a break from chemo, and then radiation—the movie *Meet Joe Black* was released. This was a modern-day story loosely based on the 1943 film *Death Takes a Holiday*. Essentially the story is about the Grim Reaper, embodied in a man named Joe Black (played by Brad Pitt), who is coming to vacation on earth in human form. While here, he befriends his next victim, billionaire mogul Bill Parrish (played by Anthony Hopkins). Joe admonishes Bill to get his earthly matters in order, because at the end of the Reaper's vacation, Bill will be coming along with him back to the afterworld. Bill resists this revelation with all his might, but ultimately comes to terms with the inevitable, and at the end of the movie he leaves peacefully with Joe.

The movie was significant to me because of the multiple extended dialogues between Joe and Bill. After seeing the movie, it became apparent to me that during my contemplative times throughout the course of my treatment, I was, in essence, having multiple conversations with my own version of Joe Black. And his message to me was always the same: "Go out and live an authentic life, as the person you truly are, or you will not survive this disease." With this bold edict, there was no room for discussion or compromise. Either I would live out the rest of my life as the woman I truly was, or I would die.

So, after surviving six months of chemotherapy and a month of radiation, and with this newfound clarity, I took Joe Black's advice and made the decision to go on hormone therapy and begin transition. I did not know what the ultimate outcome would be, but I knew I did not want to experience the other path that had been so clearly outlined by my cancer experience. When the only alternative is death, the unknown pathway becomes much more palatable.

This type of clarity is priceless. That is why having cancer was the best thing that ever happened to me.

Chapter 10

She's BACK!!!
(1998)

The next two chapters were written before I went public with my decision to transition. I completed my cancer treatments at the end of September 1998. But as expected, it took a couple months to regain my strength enough to even consider going out as Alexus. Since I was in a very contemplative place in my life, writings for my website were also temporarily suspended.

She may have been out for a few months, but she's back with a vengeance! Not only is she back, she's better, brighter, and bolder than before. And she has even changed her name from Alexandra to Alexus. For now, though, we're going to concentrate on what has changed in her psyche and her life after going through almost ten months of cancer therapy, and how she is expressing her new "attitude" to the world!

Okay, back to first person, and on with the story . . .

First of all, I didn't go out much during my treatment because I was just plain *too tired*. Even thinking about taking the time required to put on my makeup, pick out a pretty dress, and select just the right shoes made me want to take a nap. I would have saved some time on shaving my face, legs, and chest, because all my hair fell out from the chemotherapy. But unfortunately that included my eyebrows and eyelashes, so the face looking back from the mirror would not have been the beauty that any of us are used to. So I simply elected not to bother.

I went out en femme for the first time in many months in November 1998. I went with my girlfriend, Terry, and we simply went out to eat at a nice restaurant. We then went to a couple of clubs to say hi to some friends, but stayed at each place for only a few minutes and called it an early night.

The following weekend we met up with Jackie from Wyoming and went to the Hard Rock Cafe at the new Denver Pavilions Mall downtown. Once again, we made a short night of it, because my strength and endurance still aren't what they used to be. (Not to mention my feet were absolutely KILLING me from walking several blocks in heels.) I forgot how long it took me to strengthen my feet and legs for high heels when I first started dressing. But the strength *is* coming back gradually!

After those first two brief outings en femme, I met with my first Aesthetic Illusions client since before my cancer diagnosis. Barbara had come into Denver from Kansas City, and since it was going to be an all-day affair at various shops, the mall, restaurants, etc., I knew in advance I'd need comfortable shoes. So off I went to Payless Shoes for some comfortable Doc Martin knock-offs. They really do look nice with my pantsuit, and are even more comfortable than my tennis shoes. So seven hours on my feet was really no big deal—in fact, it was *fun*!!! (Thank you again, Barbara.)

MY CURRENT PERSPECTIVE
I can see early signs of identity and name integration, primarily due to the very brief section that was written in third person. I can also see that comfortable shoes are making their first appearance (wink).

At a much deeper level, there was a lot happening during this two-month hiatus. Not only was I recovering physically from the cancer treatments, I was also dealing with the emerging realization that I absolutely *must* transition. This was a truly frightening thought! I knew it would end my marriage of twenty-four years, and I didn't know if my children would be supportive. I also knew transitioning would place a great strain on my relationships with my parents, siblings, and friends. I wasn't intentionally holding back in the writings for my website, as the realities of transition were still in the formative stage in my mind. But I was literally at a precipice in my life and about to step into the void . . .

Chapter 11

Alexandra Becomes "Alexus"
(1998)

I was never really comfortable with the name Alexandra because I didn't feel like an Alexandra, even though I did like the name. I didn't really have another name in mind, and Alexandra was okay when the makeup artist came up with it, so it just sort of stuck. Since then I've been toying with other names to find one that feels better, is easier to say in casual conversation, and fits my personality. Alexus with a "u" fits me much better. There's an online website, www.kabalarians.com, that gives the personality traits of different names, and I found it very helpful. So here's the description of Alexus, which just happens to fit me to a "T" (pun intended ;-)):

> Your name of Alexus has given you an idealistic nature with a desire to help others. Your initiative often causes you to be the first to act when you see a need. Since you are impressionable and receptive, you feel the misfortunes of others very keenly. However, this name makes it awkward for you to express your deeper thoughts and feelings with finesse and diplomacy to the extent that your candid, sometimes blunt, manner of speaking creates misunderstandings with others. Being somewhat self-centered, you learn through your own experiences, as you rarely take advice from others. Yet, you are sensitive and very easily hurt and offended. You long for praise and appreciation for your efforts, but others find it difficult to understand you. You dislike monotony and system and enjoy being creative in an inventive way whether it be in interior decorating, music, art, crafts, or other endeavors that require versatility and skill. You are imaginative and visionary, somewhat of a perfectionist, yet the results of your efforts often fall short of your high expectations. A leadership position appeals to you because you would enjoy directing others rather than being directed. Your feelings are strong and you tend to react intensely to situations. Because of your sensitive nervous system, overstress and extreme tiredness could cause nervous disorders, seizures, fainting, or dizziness. You could also experience head tension such as headaches, weak eyes, or throat problems. (www.kabalarians.com)

I think this fits me very well, and I have already received many compliments on the new name. I will gradually be changing the pages of my website to fit my new identity, but in the meantime, you will have to excuse the two-name schizophrenia.

MY CURRENT PERSPECTIVE

Changing your name is a very powerful exercise in self-discovery. Choosing a name for a newborn, as we did for our two daughters, is difficult enough, but choosing a name for yourself as an adult is an entirely different matter. I felt the need to find a name that preserved the energy and the good memories of who I had been, yet at the same time left room for the new and uplifting feminine energy that was just starting to express itself in me.

I was able to choose my new first name after just a few weeks of contemplation and online name searching. But choosing my last name was much more difficult. I tried and tried, using the same techniques as I had with my first name, but there are no books on choosing surnames. As a result, I decided to stop struggling and simply turned it over to the Universe, knowing the answer would come in due time.

I got the answer about two or three weeks later. I was driving my car through a nearby suburb and wasn't thinking about anything in particular, and just as I crested a hill after going through a busy intersection, the name literally dropped out of the sky: I heard a booming voice, which came from above and behind me, clearly say the name, "Sheppard . . . S H E P P A R D!"

Hmm, I thought. *Alexus Sheppard . . . I really like the sound of that.* Interestingly enough, to this very day, when using a personal check or credit card, I often get compliments on my name. That makes me feel good!

> *Note: The decision to change my last name came concurrently with my decision to transition. This was for two specific reasons. First, I wanted to protect my youngest daughter, who was still in middle school. Knowing that middle school can sometimes be a cruel place, I didn't want anyone to recognize my last name when I was out in public and then somehow*

have this information filter back to Erika's school and cause problems for her there. Secondly, since my parents were not yet being supportive of my transition, changing my last name was a way to emphasize the conviction of my decision and create distance from them.

PART TWO

Transitional Phase

(1998–2000)

November 1998　　　　　　July 2000

My transitional phase began in December 1998. I had recently completed nine months of chemotherapy and radiation for Hodgkin's disease, and in the months immediately following had spent a great deal of time in prayer and meditation. As a result of that introspection I was inspired to begin living authentically, go on hormones, have cosmetic feminization surgery, begin my real-life experience (RLE), legally change my name, and initiate the required psychotherapy to get my letters for sexual reassignment surgery (SRS), which is now called gender confirmation surgery (GCS).

I also knew that decision would end my marriage of twenty-four years.

This section will be a collection of writings and pictures from that period.

Chapter 12

Transsexual and Not Just CD?
(1999)

This piece was originally written very early in 1999. At that point in life I was still married and living in Denver with my wife and children.

This was one of the most difficult yet most exciting realizations of my life. One does not go through many months of treatment for a life-threatening illness without doing some major soul-searching. To say that I have come out of those treatments a changed person would be an understatement.

First of all, I have discovered that I am not afraid of dying. I have always known of my Spiritual source, and am even more aware of it now. When death does come along, I know it will be just another transition from this form to another. If birth is a miracle of life, is not death just as miraculous an event? The fact that we cannot "see" what is on the other side only wraps it in superstition and religious dogma.

Once I came to the realization that death really has no power over us other than what we give it, I had to come to terms with an age-old question: "What is the meaning of life?"

For me, the answer to that question was, "To thine own heart be true." In the simplest terms that means I intend to spend the rest of this lifetime living my life to the absolute fullest. That does not mean that I will run roughshod over the hearts or feelings of others; it just means that their desires will no longer take precedence over mine. I have lived my entire life according to the rules and expectations of my family, my profession, my childhood, society, my friends, and more. Those days are over! It is time to get on with my life.

Most people are dealing with their own issues. To assume that they somehow have insight as to how we should live *our* lives is to assign them supernatural powers that they simply do not possess. They may well have ideas about how we should fit into their ideals of how a life should look, but ultimately those ideas are about them, not us. The question to ask yourself is, "What feels right in my heart, today, right now?" The present moment is *all* we have! We all plan for tomorrow, next week, next year, and decades to come, and to some extent that is okay. But the reality is, those days may never arrive for us. So to sacrifice the reality of today for the possibility of tomorrow is to give away our life.

I knew from the very first time I saw myself in the mirror en femme that I was looking at the "real" me. Even though I have continued, since that fateful day, to attempt to fit the mold of the "typical crossdresser," deep down I have known from the very beginning that I am a transsexual. The deep-seated relief of that realization is something that cannot be put into words. Along with that realization comes the conflict of my responsibilities to my family, profession, and society. But I have decided to give those things the secondary billing they deserve. This is my life, and it ain't no dress rehearsal!

Now comes the need to begin hormone replacement therapy and electrolysis. I am completely aware that taking full doses of prescription-strength female hormones will change my body completely and permanently. I am not only willing but also excited to live with those changes. I also know that there are friends and family members who will never understand why I am doing this, but I hope most of them will at least be willing to try to get to know the new me. The "old" me died with the cancer, and the person who now lives in this body has a new set of rules. She is more loving and compassionate than he could ever be. She is more alive and energetic than he ever wanted to be. She likes to dance, party, and be out with her friends, while he was quite content to stay at home. She cries easily and frequently, while he was often either emotionally unavailable or angry. There is nothing he could do that she cannot do, but there are lots of things she can do that he could not! A friend in the community recently summed it up by saying she is not "instead of him, but rather, in addition to him." I like that analogy.

As you might imagine, what I'm going through is quite difficult for my wife and youngest daughter. My oldest daughter, meanwhile, is seemingly fine with the news of my imminent transition. My wife and I have discussed this in depth, on many occasions, and have decided to stay together as long as possible. She doesn't know if she can live with another woman full-time or not, but she is willing to give it a try, as much as humanly possible, in order to maintain our twenty-eight-year relationship. She has already seen changes in who I am as a result of the hormones, and for the most part likes the mellowing of attitude she's seen. I still live most of the time in drab (dressed as a man) but am spending more and more time en femme when the family's busy schedule will allow it.

I am trying to minimize the impact this transition will have on my youngest daughter by being sensitive to her middle school social calendar. She still has lots of friends over to visit after school and on weekends, only now she makes sure I know well in advance when that will happen. My oldest daughter is in college, so isn't impacted as directly, and since she is a very open-minded, free spirit, I don't expect her to have any major problems with my transition. I hope I've made it clear that regardless of my physical condition or state of dress, I'll always be their "Daddy."

The next few months, and years, will be interesting, to say the least. The difference is, I am now living my life from heart, not from mind.

MY CURRENT PERSPECTIVE
This writing is one of the more in-depth and emotionally honest pieces thus far. I think that's because I had just completed many months of cancer treatments and was still at a very introspective time in my life. I had also made the decision to begin transitioning, so there was no need to continue the act of pretending to be something I was not. That was a very freeing experience. Once the façade is gone, all that remains is the authentic self. There is no need for bravado or exaggerated public self.

I have also noticed a significant difference in these introspective writings as compared with those that have a more entertaining feel to them. It is almost as if one style is real, and the other style is for show, with the authentic self still being safely held in reserve.

What this piece failed to truly address was the ever-increasing likelihood of divorce I was facing. Even though my ex was desperately trying to keep our marriage intact, she simply wasn't interested in a relationship with another woman. She had told me from our very earliest conversations about my taking hormones that there would be only one pair of breasts in our bed (and she already had them). So as I came to terms with my needing to transition, I was also coming to terms with the realization that our marriage was almost certainly going to end. She was sincerely trying to come to terms with the realities of my transition, but I think we both knew that the end of our marriage was almost inevitable.

Chapter 13

Being "Out There"
(1998)

So what's all this about Alexus spreading her wings? Well, since my recovery from cancer, my femme psyche has become obsessed with being "out there." How is the world going to know about transgender people if we all stay home in the closet, or only go to gay/lesbian clubs and restaurants? So with the holiday season coming up, what better time to get dressed to the nines and kick up my heels?

As you may remember, I am a licensed Religious Science Practitioner (spiritual counselor). Every Christmas we have a Practitioner/Minister Christmas party at the church. It is usually attended by about a hundred people, with practitioners, ministers, spouses and significant others. People who attend Mile Hi Church are, for the most part, a very loving, liberal-thinking, and non-judgmental group. We also have a very active LGBT support group within the church, and there are a couple of trans women who occasionally attend our services (though none are practitioners or regular attendees). As a result, the practitioners and ministers are shining examples of how to live the philosophy of unconditional love and acceptance.

So, Alexus decided to make this Christmas event her "coming out" party! After all, what "straight" function could I possibly attend that would be safer?

I decided to wear the infamous "LBD" (little black dress) for the event. But one must have SOME color, so I made an appointment at a local nail shop for some nice acrylic nails—with a festive holiday airbrush design, of course. They turned out very nice, with red polish and a white peppermint cane with a green bow. I thought my pretty nails would nicely compliment my LBD, black patent shoes, black hose, long blond hair, and red lipstick.

I dressed casual en femme for the nail appointment, and was treated very nicely by the nail technician and other women in the shop.

Okay, okay, now on to the main event . . .

The party was an evening buffet, starting at 6 P.M. I knew I wanted to be fashionably late, by about fifteen minutes. And wouldn't you know it—it started to snow at about 5 P.M. So I got to walk through about two inches of fresh snow and ice (a great trick on four-inch stiletto heels) to get to the door from my car when I parked at the church around 6:15. My heart was pounding so loudly I'm surprised they didn't hear me coming; I haven't been that nervous since the very first night I went out as Alexandra! And at least then I knew I was going to be surrounded entirely by other transgender sisters. This was going to be *very different* from that night.

I paused for a moment for a brief prayer to summon the Loving Feminine Energy of the Universe before walking into the church.

The very first person I met in the hallway was one of the most loving women I know. She had been one of the teachers in a practitioner class I'd taken, and needless to say, she didn't recognize me. I called out to her and "introduced" myself, and after she recovered from the initial shock, she asked me "What's going on?"

I quickly explained my transgender nature, and told her that my feminine side had been uncovered during one of my later practitioner classes. Even though she had previously been unaware of my being transgender, she was very accepting, gave me a hug, and said she'd be there for me if at any time I needed her help during the evening.

I walked into the meeting room and attempted to sign my name—no small task with brand-new long nails, and hands that were shaking from nervousness. I was instantly spotted by some of my classmates who had met "her" before, and was immediately surrounded by a loving and caring, although very surprised, group of wonderful people. They all wanted to know why I had come to the party en femme, but seemed unbothered once I explained the reason.

I went to a table and attempted to pour myself a glass of wine, but my hands were shaking so badly that I only poured half a glass before stopping, knowing full well I'd only spill it if I filled it to a normal measure.

Even before I could finish my half glass of wine, the lady who had initially greeted me in the hallway came over to tell me she had sent up a silent prayer for an evening of peace and loving acceptance. I was instantly soothed by both her love and the love of Spirit within the room.

Once my nervousness began to subside, I began to enjoy the conversation and loving energy of my friends. I discovered that I am *truly* unrecognizable en femme—something I had always thought to be true, but wasn't entirely sure about until this party. I was "read" and identified by only one person who knew my male side. She made the connection on her own, even though she had never met Alexus before. I believe this is because she is a massage therapist, so is very familiar with the natural movements of men vs. women, and knew immediately I was not what I appeared to be. But she was also very loving, and totally supportive of my being there as Alexus.

I spent most of the evening "introducing" myself to the rest of my former classmates and a select group of other practitioners who did not know of my femme side. Even after they knew who I was, most of them simply could not believe that it was really me. I literally had to approach them individually, call them by name, and put my arm around them to get their attention. Most of them simply thought I was the significant other of one of the practitioners, and wondered who I came to the party with and why I was being so friendly to everyone.

It was a delightful, loving, fun evening, once I got my heart to stop pounding—one I will certainly never forget! (And nor will a few other people.)

MY CURRENT PERSPECTIVE
This piece has definitely gone back to the entertainment style of writing. There is also a lot of back and forth between first and third person. This will probably persist throughout most of my transitional writings. Since I was still living most of the time as male, this period was very complicated and difficult. As time went along, I gradually moved from presenting mostly as male to presenting mostly as female. It will be interesting to see if the writing style changes toward the end of this period.

Even though there are significant descriptions in this piece regarding how frightened I was to attend this function en femme, there truly are not words that can adequately describe the inner terror I felt as I walked into the church that night. I was excited to begin a new chapter in my life, but at the same time, every cell in my egocentric being screamed, "Don't do it! Turn around! Go back! You're going to DIE!!!" And from the way my heart was pounding, I thought I just might.

This would be a moment in time from which I would never recover. Good or bad, there was no turning back. My life would never be the same. Other authors have called these moments "stepping into the void." What a fantastic description that is! Into the void I went . . .

As I look back on this moment from today's perspective, I am amazed that I actually had the courage to make that high-heeled walk through the snowy church parking lot that night. But at the same time, I realize that my cancer experience had given me the courage and realization that there truly was no choice. When you're faced with making a difficult decision but know the only alternative is actual physical death, the decision suddenly doesn't seem so difficult.

Chapter 14

Alexus Goes to Church
(1998)

Okay, I'll admit, it all started with these pretty Christmas nails. If you read my last story, you already know that I had my nails done for a Saturday night church Christmas party. That party went so well, and I felt so pretty and festive, I just couldn't bring myself to remove my new nails after just one wearing. I thought about just going shopping at the mall, but decided instead to spread my wings a little more. I decided to go to church en femme!

And since it is the Christmas season, what better time to wear my nice red Gantos coatdress? I knew that red would not exactly "blend in" without attracting some attention, but then, Alexus *thrives* on attention, so what the heck! I also knew that there would be lots of other women in attendance that would be wearing the seasonal red, green, or otherwise festive apparel, so I didn't think I'd look out of place.

The courage for this bold move came from the absolute acceptance I'd felt at the party the night before. But everyone at that party was a licensed Religious Science practitioner or minister, and had been trained to be non-judgmental and accepting of others. While Mile Hi Church is known for being very liberal and free-thinking, like any other church, there are people in attendance who can "walk the talk" and some who can't. So I was a little nervous about attending a service with 900 people, most of whom didn't know anything about the transgender community. And since we have back-to-back services, there would be another 900 people coming for the next service as I was standing in the lobby chatting with friends and introducing myself to many of them for the first time. I saw it as another opportunity to grow and learn to be comfortable with who I really am.

The result of the morning was very similar to the night before, in that I was now completely confident that I was totally unrecognizable as my male self. If I didn't walk up to people and introduce myself, nobody raised an eyebrow (other than in admiration). And this gave me the opportunity to introduce many friends to Alexus who had not yet had the chance to meet her.

As I was standing in the main lobby chatting with some of my friends, one of my close lady friends who has known about Alexus since the beginning had a particularly fun time watching the men walk by and "check me out." I really don't usually notice such things, but I was standing with my back to the main traffic flow, and she was able to glance past me to watch the reactions. I think she was having as much fun as I was.

Another lady who didn't know of my femme side was introduced to Alexus by a mutual friend. She was then asked if I reminded her of anyone. She had that puzzled look on her face, and then said I looked like I could be Allen's (my male name) sister. I smiled, our mutual friend laughed, and then I told her I was a lot closer to him than just being his sister. Needless to say, she was surprised and flabbergasted, but totally accepting once we were properly introduced. Another positive reinforcement of being unrecognizable . . .

MY CURRENT PERSPECTIVE
I remember how exciting this period was! I was finally able to express myself as the woman I was deep down inside. I was finally living, albeit only part-time, as the woman who had been hidden away for so very long. It felt like Christmas every day I got to live en femme. So it is only natural that these writings have the energy of excitement. These experiences gave me somewhat the same feeling as a young girl who's just been asked out for her first date or invited to the prom. Every day was a new adventure and a new experience. I finally got to see the world through authentic eyes! I could choose to share my past identity or not, as I was readily passing as the woman I knew myself to be. That was such a wonderful feeling, the feeling of simply being whole and authentic.

I was also getting confirmation from people who were not a part of the LGBT community about how pretty I was. This was both exciting and validating. It was a real boost for my confidence level and helped diminish any feelings of trepidation, especially regarding my ability to move through mainstream society without being seen as a man in a dress. There is a significant difference between the idea of going out in public on a regular basis, in the relative safety of the cross-dressing community, and living a normal, day-to-day life as a full-time woman. I finally had external validation that this was, indeed, possible.

I also realize that my transition experience was not necessarily the same experience that other transgender women may have. Some would go as far as to say that my experience was fairly atypical because I pass so easily. While this is wonderful in my day-to-day life, I do sometimes have some guilt about this.

(As mentioned in earlier chapters, Chapter 32 of this book is devoted entirely to the subject of passing.)

Chapter 15

Writings
(1999)

February 1999 Update
As I've remodeled my website several times throughout the years, I've sometimes been accused of "sanitizing" my site. Now, when looking back over my old pages, I will readily admit that was true. As I evolved from CD to TG and then to TS, I felt my site needed to be reflective of who I thought I was at that given moment. Therefore, as I changed, so did my website. But when I did that, even though my intentions were good, the new pages lost their historical reference and therefore their potential relevance to others still struggling with the issues I'd faced. Unfortunately, some of my earliest website index files, written in early 1997, were rewritten, overwritten, and/or simply replaced as the later evolutions came along. Fortunately, most of the stories and pictures survived, and I was able to resurrect them (and they're included in this book with minimal editing).

June 1999 Update
On April 21st, 1999, I had thirteen hours of cosmetic surgery done. I had a face lift, brow lift, eyelid lift, lip injections, neck

lift, Adam's apple removal, stomach and love handle liposuction, and tummy tuck. I have recovered nicely, and continue to look better almost every day.

So far my waist is down 3 ½ inches, and it continues to get smaller as the last bit of swelling goes away. My face looks about twenty years younger, and my lips now have that nice "pouty" look.

October 1999 Update
About Alexus:
At first, from late 1996 through 1997, I considered myself a GEM (Gender Enhanced Male). I used that term because I thought it was more descriptive than crossdresser, and less clinical than transvestite. But I definitely knew that I was a transgender male of some sort. I had a real "gut feeling" from the very first night I saw "her" in the mirror that I might be transsexual, but could not even begin to explore that possibility until I tried out the less dramatic forms of transgender expression. But none of them felt like the "real me." So with the help of a *lot* of introspection, a year of cancer treatment, and a little psychotherapy, I came to the following conclusion:

I am a forty-seven-year-old pre-op MTF transsexual (meaning I had not yet had Gender Confirmation Surgery). I am currently living full-time as a woman and have been on hormones since January 1999. I am relatively new to the gender community, as I only began exploring my femme persona in December of 1996. I think getting in touch with my feminine side is the best thing that has ever happened to me. It has made me a better person in all aspects of my life.

November 23, 1999 Update
In May of 1999, my wife and I decided to get a divorce. The divorce was a "friendly" divorce, as we had been married for twenty-four years and we have two wonderful daughters

together. Quite simply, we came to the conclusion that we could no longer live together as man and wife. (I had come to the realization that I could no longer live my life as a man and she did not want to remain in a marriage with a transitioning transsexual woman.) As a result, I will be moving as a single woman into a new condo in February 2000, when it's finished. In the meantime, I continue to live at home with my ex-spouse as my landlord and roommate. (She got the house as part of the divorce agreement.)

I have legally changed both my name and gender. I live 24/7 as Alexus now; my real-life experience continues. I am planning to get sexual reassignment surgery sometime within the next year. But before that happens, I will need to settle into my new condo, get it all furnished and decorated, and enjoy some time as a single professional woman.

Life for me has taken so many interesting twists and turns; I can barely scratch the surface with these brief descriptions. My main hope is that some of you reading this will be inspired to follow your own pathway to expression of the heart, and will become as happy as I am. God bless each and every one of you, as She certainly has blessed me.

MY CURRENT PERSPECTIVE
1999 was a pivotal year for me. It was the year after my cancer experience and officially marked the beginning of my transition. Since I was very busy with all the physical, social, and legal necessities of transition, the time I spent writing and expanding my website was extremely limited. That is the reason for the brief and infrequent updates.

The first section, which discusses the evolution of my website throughout the years, came as a result of being challenged by one of my long-time readers. When I first started my website I simply wanted an online outlet for my writings. I wrote the initial pages as an unofficial blog/journal of my transgender journey, with no intention of it becoming anything more. As the months went by, however, I became increasingly aware of how popular my pages had become. I was new to the transgender community and had no previous experience in either writing or designing a website. I had no idea that in a matter of months, I would become somewhat of an online "celebrity" within the community. I think this is primarily due to the fact that I passed relatively easily and posted lots of photos along with my stories.

As my definition of self evolved, I began to modify my website to fit those changes. I had no idea that anyone would care, and I was becoming uncomfortable with some of my earlier writings. As I have said already, I find the energy and tone of the early writings overly masculine and sometimes misogynistic. I think that writing style was likely due to the many decades of overcompensation and denial of anything feminine within me, as well as my early denial that I might actually be transsexual.

So, as I began to change my transgender expression, I altered my website to fit my newfound perspective. As I did, I was immediately challenged by some of my readers and accused of trying to hide my cross-dressing past. In retrospect, I can now admit that they were absolutely correct.

Unfortunately, there is a distinct hierarchy and social separation between those who identify as drag queens, fetish-driven transvestites, crossdressers, and transsexuals. There is further separation between transsexuals who are M2F, F2M, pre-op, post-op, or non-op. And these categories don't even take into account those who are gender fluid or genderqueer. But it is beyond the scope of this book to adequately explain or significantly explore the nearly infinite variations of gender expression. I am simply describing my own personal experiences and ever-evolving viewpoint—and also acknowledging that as I moved through the various transgender expressions,

I unfortunately modified and/or deleted some of the writings that made me uncomfortable at that moment.

The cosmetic surgery I had done in April of 1999 was meant to feminize my face and body so I could live and move more easily within society as the woman I was becoming. The surgery took thirteen hours, and when I awoke, I looked as if a bus had hit me. Actually, that's pretty much how I felt too. I was on muscle relaxants and narcotic pain meds for two weeks.

Many M2F women also have what is called facial feminization surgery (FFS). My surgery did not fall into that exact category, as I didn't really need much facial bone recontouring. FFS is typically done to reshape heavy brow bones, soften the angle of the jaw, reshape the chin and nose, and alter whatever other facial characteristics appear stereotypically male on a given person. It is literally feminizing the part of the skull that is the foundation for the face.

My initial surgery did not include gender confirmation surgery, as that would come much later. Even though society seems to be fixated on the state of a transsexual person's genitals, the feminization surgery is much more important in day-to-day living throughout the requisite real life experience (RLE) and post-transition life. Very few people see your genitals, but everyone sees your face and overall body shape, and can sense your level of self-confidence. Genitals have nothing to do with 99 percent of your life and certainly do not define gender.

* * *

My fall writings from 1999 are primarily announcements that I was in the process of getting a divorce and had begun my RLE. At that point I had legally changed my name and gotten a new driver's license with the gender marked as female. At that pre-9/11 time in Colorado, changing your legal gender marker required only a letter from your doctor or therapist and a new picture.

I was in the process of doing the required therapy to get my letters for gender confirmation surgery during that time. I was also trying to complete any and all business that might require a personal appearance in male mode, since, after nearly a year on hormones and with the nice result from my feminization surgery, it was becoming increasingly difficult for me to pass as a man. What a strange and exciting time that was!

Chapter 16

Erika's Story
(1999)

This story was written by my youngest daughter, Erika, in 2001, when she was sixteen years old. It has always been one of the most popular pages of my website, so I wanted to include it here. She is now thirty-one years old and a successful professional dancer, and lives in Las Vegas.

It was almost like any other night . . .
. . . except for this nervous feeling that I had in my stomach. I'd had the feeling for a while that my parents might be getting a divorce, but I didn't really want to believe it. Actually, the thought of them being divorced didn't bother me as much as the fact that I didn't want to have to live in two different houses. I didn't have dance that night so I was just going to hang around the house and play on my computer, but I just couldn't get this nervous feeling out of my stomach. My mom came into my room and told me that my dad and she needed to talk to me. Right away I knew what was coming. I just knew that they were going to be getting a divorce and I would have to live in two different houses. I just knew it. So we walked into

the kitchen and sat down at the table. I remember wanting to cry, but knew that for some reason I had to be strong. I was just waiting to hear that small little word, "divorce," but they didn't speak of it. Instead a picture album was placed in front of me. I had no idea what was in the photo album, I only knew that it had to be better than hearing my parents telling me they were getting a divorce.

I opened up the photo album and the first picture was of a lady singing in a sparkly formal dress. I didn't know what was happening, so I kept looking through the pictures, and they all were of this lady that I had never seen before. I don't think that either of my parents said anything until I was completely done looking through all the pictures. My dad was sitting to the left of me and my mom was sitting across the table. My dad opened up the album to the first picture again, and I will remember these next words for the rest of my life. As I was staring at this picture of a lady singing, my dad said, "That's me."

The rest of the night was spent basically explaining to me that, in the past, my dad would occasionally dress up and go sing as a woman. But now, my dad was going to begin transition into BECOMING a woman. The only thing that I could think of was, *Thank goodness they aren't getting a divorce.* We talked about all of the options that were ahead of us, and how we were going to take this whole thing day by day. So that is exactly what I did: I took it day by day, and every day that something didn't directly involve me, I acted as if nothing had ever happened.

I decided that the "stubborn approach" was going to be the way I handled the whole thing. I kept myself busy with school and dance so that I wouldn't have to be around the house or deal with what was actually going on. This worked for a little while, until my dad got more serious about living and dressing as a woman, and I got more serious about being a stubborn teenager. Also, in the midst of me being at dance all the time and my sister moving away to college, my parents decided that they were going to get a divorce, though this was something they wanted to take slowly so that neither of them lost anything unfairly. Of course, the first question out of my mouth when they finally told me about the decision was custody and who was I going to live with. I was informed that they were not going to go through the whole court system and I would just decide who I was going to live with.

However, at this point my dad was not going to move out of the house until a new condo being built nearby was finished. So, I was just going to continue living in my house and acting like nothing was happening.

The hardest thing about what my dad was doing was the fact that I was trying to keep it a secret from everyone. I had always had the "All American" perfect family, and I wanted to keep it that way. However, at that moment the Tomlinson household was anything but perfect. I was in middle school, and every child finds middle school awkward enough, let alone dealing with trying to hide your father from your friends when you come home from school. That was always my biggest issue, because as I said before, if I acted like nothing was happening, maybe it wouldn't. But, I also knew that a lady slightly resembling my dad and always hanging around the house might bring unwanted attention by my friends. On a daily basis I would come home from school and have friends with me or want to bring friends over and my dad would be dressed in women's clothes sitting in the kitchen. So we would argue about it, or I would try and sneak my friends into my room without them seeing. The situation was definitely not working, so I knew that I had to tell someone.

★ ★ ★

I was in 8th grade, in Mr. Gillian's science class; we were taking notes and getting ready to just have time to study on our own. I was sitting next to my friend Annaleigh in the back of the room, sort of paying attention. We knew that if we talked quietly Mr. Gillian wouldn't yell at us, because he liked us both. (He and his wife used to ballroom dance, so with Annaleigh and I both being dancers, that created a common ground for us all.) That year I was close to a lot of my teachers. Annaleigh and I would talk about everything, but that day after taking notes I knew that I had to tell her and that she would not judge me or alienate me, and most of all I knew that she would understand and care. I have absolutely no idea how I told her, but I remember just breaking down and crying to her in the back of science class. The rest of the day was a blur, as was most of the year. Actually, I only have a few vivid memories that included my dad until this issue came along.

When I turned sixteen, some things started to click in my life. I had my own car, so that gave me a sense of freedom; I could escape and go to dance, which was my equivalent to therapy. I would drive over to my dad's condo every once in a while and clean or just hang out. One of my favorite things about the condo was when my dad subscribed to WAM TV, a totally random kids' network that I had landed a dancing commercial on. I remember the first day we watched the stupidest shows just to see my commercial. That was so special and still makes me smile just to think about us sitting there. We had started to become friends more than father and daughter, because trying to have a typical father/daughter relationship wouldn't work. The thing that my dad still says to me to this day, and that I absolutely love is, "Erika, I will always be your dad and I will always love you."

Friendship was definitely the common ground. Things were going well and I was accepting my dad more and more every day. I had good friends at school, and I had finally reached the point where I didn't care what people thought about my dad or me. If they could not accept this part of my life, they could no longer be my friends. Thankfully, I didn't lose any of my friends over the situation. All of my close friends knew and the rest of the school was slowly starting to find out. People never really approached me about it, but I just had this sense, especially with all my teachers, that they already knew. Telling my friends was getting easier, but I still didn't really have a good way of telling the story. Without fail, every time I would start to talk about it, I would cry. I found this odd, as I thought that I was okay with it, and starting to accept it, but I couldn't help crying every time I talked about it. I see now, that like I had done most of my life, I just hid any painful feelings I had and moved on.

★ ★ ★

In October 2001, five months after my sixteenth birthday, my dad had been in Montreal, Canada, for gender reassignment surgery and was getting ready to come back home. I never really asked much about what exactly was going to happen in the surgery, but I knew the basics. I decided that I wanted to do something special for my dad, because this was a big, exciting step in her life. I went and bought some decorations, not just ordinary ones but "It's A Girl" baby decorations. I went over and decorated the whole condo and it looked cute. I had to go run some errands but I was going to come back later when my dad got home. I was so proud of my decorations and so excited to see my dad's reaction.

As soon as I was done with my errands I went back to the condo. I walked in and there was my dad, crying because she was so happy to see me and loved the decorations that I had put up. She came over and gave me a hug, and for the first time ever in my life hugging my dad felt really weird. So I made up this excuse that I had to be home for something and got out of there as fast as I could. I went directly home and straight to the bathroom floor, where I cried until my mom came home.

My mom and I talked all night long about how I was feeling and decided that what was coming up for me were all of the emotions I had never shared with anyone else and had kept bottled up inside me, that were now coming out full force. I was also realizing for the first time that I would never have a "normal" dad. The thought of this bothered me for days, and I couldn't stop crying. I was crying over everything that I had tried to ignore when I first found out about it all. I hated that my dad would never be able to walk me down the aisle; I hated that my boyfriends would never be afraid of my dad; but most of all I hated myself for not being able to just accept all of this and move on. So in an attempt to move on, I started pulling away and was going over to the condo a lot less and falling back into my patterns of just acting like nothing was wrong and hiding my emotions.

This year, 2001, was senior year in high school, and I decided to take a psychology class taught by Mrs. Rossie. The class was first semester of my senior year, and I was so excited to take it. I had some of my good girlfriends in the class with me as well. Within the first week, Mrs. Rossie handed out our first assignment. The assignment was to create a road map of your life. You had to have fifteen street signs, or locations, on your map that represented fifteen big parts of your life. I loved the project and was so excited to complete it!

The due date came and we all turned in our maps, and then Mrs. Rossie popped a surprise on us: over the next few days, we would be sharing three of the major events on our road maps. I can remember sitting on the back couch with five of my girlfriends when she said this and my heart stopped beating. I knew what I should share with the class, but I didn't know if I could do it. I didn't talk to anyone about what I would share, but I knew what I had to do.

The day that I had to present my road map and the three significant events, I was actually nervous, and I hadn't been nervous for a long time. But I stood up and I did it. I stood there in front of five of my best friends, thirty other peers who were acquaintances of mine, and a teacher I wasn't very close to, and started to tell my story. I remember seeing people's mouths drop, but I kept going. I actually made it through the whole story with almost no tears. That day my teacher came up to me and told me how much she admired my bravery and my strength. I don't know exactly why, but somehow telling my story to people I hardly knew, and then hearing what my teacher had to say afterwards, made a huge difference in my life.

Today, I can tell the story of my dad and me to anyone without crying. I think that means that I have truly come to peace with it all, and have truly achieved 100 percent full acceptance of my dad. I just hope that someday I can return all of the love she has given to me, and show her how much I love her and appreciate everything that she has done for me. The direction that our life has decided to take us in has made us the people that we are today, and that couldn't make me any happier to be me and have her as my dad!

Thank you for making me the person that I am today. I love you.

—Erika

MY CURRENT PERSPECTIVE
It was wonderful when Erika wrote this letter, and it's still wonderful today! I know it has helped many, many people.

After she wrote this piece, I asked Erika when she finally became okay with my transition. I was expecting a response involving something dramatic or complex, so I was quite surprised by her answer. She simply said, "I became okay with your transition when I finally realized that *you* were going to be okay." How profound and perfect!

Chapter 17

Thirty-Year High School Class Reunion
(2000)

From the very first notification of my thirtieth class reunion, I knew I wanted to attend. As you may have gathered from my other stories, my transgender experience is very much a journey of Spirit, not ego. I did not want to attend the reunion for vanity reasons, but rather to educate and inform. Most straight (and cisgender) people have never met a transgender person, and this is especially true in small towns. If we all stay in the closet or live in complete stealth mode, the negative attitudes and prejudices toward us will never change. And if fully transitioned transsexuals simply move on with their new lives without making contacts from the past, the result is the same: no education . . . no chance for change in societal attitudes.

I am from a very small, rural town in Kansas. The population of the entire town is only about two thousand people, and my graduating class had only sixty-six students. I was voted "Outstanding Graduating Senior" by the high school faculty. I lettered all four years in track, music, and scholastics, and two years in football. I was also in the National Honor Society and won a statewide public speaking contest, so my high school experience was anything but low profile.

As I began to seriously contemplate attending the reunion, I asked my parents for their consent for me to attend my reunion (as Alexus, of course). They are both in their seventies and still live in that small, conservative, rural town. I knew I could easily come to the reunion, make my appearance, and return to Denver with little permanent impact on my personal life (since Denver is hundreds of miles away). But since they still lived there, I knew they would have to live with the aftermath of such a public appearance.

While they did have some reservations, they agreed that if I truly wanted to attend, I should.

From the day I sent in my registration, I began sending e-mails and snail mails to some of my classmates. I wanted my new name and transgender status to be common knowledge before I arrived. I thought this would minimize the impact on the reunion activities and allow people to at least start dealing with their issues beforehand. Within a couple of days, I was the "talk of the town" in the local coffee shops. My mother called to relay this information to me, and I can't say I was surprised. But gossip notwithstanding, I received seven supportive letters from classmates before the event.

My girlfriend at that time, Cristina, agreed to lend moral support by going with me to the reunion. Since we are both licensed Spiritual Counselors, we made sure we were "prayed up" before our arrival. She grew up in a large city, so this was to be her first experience with small-town life, attitudes, and people.

In a word, the reunion went fabulously! Believe it or not,

there was not a single negative event concerning my attendance as a woman. There were a few people who were standoffish or simply didn't want to approach us, but nobody came up to me and made any negative comments! In fact, the opposite occurred. I had several people from other classes go out of their way to walk up to me and say how proud they were of my having the courage to attend. Isn't that absolutely amazing?

There were twenty-six classmates in attendance from our original class of sixty-six people (a very decent showing!). We attended four events: two open houses at private homes, the all-school banquet at the high school, and a night of dancing at a new nightclub in town.

I have no doubt that I was the "talk of the town" in the coffee shops again after the reunion. I also assume there was some negative talk, half-truths, and probably even some outright lies about what people saw, or chose *not* to see, in my new persona. But people will be people, and as long as they keep their prejudices and bigotry to themselves, they can think anything they wish—and they will.

All in all, it went better than I could have *ever* dreamed! When in doubt, follow your heart . . .

MY CURRENT PERSPECTIVE

When I originally wrote this piece, I intentionally failed to mention that my parents were still struggling with my transition. So everything wasn't quite as perfect as I made it sound here. While it was true that there were no overt negative reactions from the other reunion attendees, the same could not be said for the energy in my parents' household.

When Cristina and I would come home from an event quite excited about how accepting everyone had been, it felt almost as if my parents were somehow disappointed that we hadn't been shamed or treated poorly by someone. I think since they were not yet personally comfortable with my transition, they were hoping someone else would demonstrate negative feelings towards us to mirror their own. Cristina and I discussed this repeating pattern of negativity—how we came home from multiple events feeling excited and happy, only to be treated with the energy of disappointment when we came through the door at my parents' home.

To their credit, I think my parents were trying to be as supportive as they possibly could. Still, deep down inside, they were hoping someone at the reunion would somehow convince me to stop my transition and go back to how things "used to be." They had no grasp on the reality that going back to living in male mode as Allen would absolutely physically kill me.

In many ways, however, they were being forced into a transition of their own. They needed to transition from having what they considered to be a completely normal, white, conservative, midwestern, Republican, Christian home to something that from their perspective was quite abnormal. And this was all being done without their consent and out of their control. So of course there was some resistance. I didn't understand this at the time; looking back, though, I can clearly see that they were in their own transitional pain. This current-day perspective gives me some compassion for what they were experiencing.

Since this piece was written I have attended three additional class reunions. Everyone in my class is still very supportive, and in fact my transition is now simply "old news." The recent Caitlin Jenner publicity has raised some additional questions and comparisons from a few classmates, but everything remains quite positive.

My parents have come along quite nicely too. They almost never use the wrong pronoun anymore, and when they do, it is quite obvious it was unintentional. They have accepted me as the daughter they didn't know they had, and are genuinely loving toward me and my wife, Deb. Transitions always take time to mature—for all of us.

Chapter 18

Gender Confirmation Surgery
(2001)

Although my GCS was performed in October 2001, and I continued to have an intermittent Internet website presence for many years following, I never actually wrote at length about my surgery. This omission was for a variety of reasons. First and foremost, by the time I finally had my surgery, I had been living full-time as Alexus for over two years. So for me, the surgery was somewhat anticlimactic. Secondly, as I continued to live a busy and authentic life as the woman I had become, I took my website offline. While the journaling had been cathartic for me as I made my way through my transgender journey, after transition that need no longer existed. And I simply didn't want to invest the time writing what felt like a "final chapter" story.

As it turned out, that "final" event was just the beginning of my new life.

As a result of my decision not to write about this experience sooner, this chapter is written from my current (2015) perspective, based on memories of my experience almost fourteen years ago. Since this timetable is being reconstructed entirely from memory, the exact timing of individual events may be slightly different from other similar reports. Keep in mind as well that it is not intended to be used as a guide for current-day surgical follow-up.

* * *

Our society has a long-standing fascination with the status of a transgender person's genitals. We've seen this portrayed in the media since Christine Jorgensen made front-page headlines back in 1952 in the *New York Daily News*, which declared, "Ex-GI Becomes Blonde Bombshell." This sensationalist headline was a result of her having a "Sex Change Operation" while in Europe. In reality, she hadn't had just one surgery but rather a series of procedures, most of which were performed in Denmark between 1951 and 1952. She returned to the US in 1953 and became an instant celebrity.

Although Jorgensen was incorrectly described as the first person to have gender reassignment surgery (similar procedures had been performed in Europe as early as the late 1920s and early 1930s), it is true that she was the first person to have hormone therapy combined with those surgeries. And she was certainly the first transgender American to hit the mass media.

Transgender people have lived amongst us since the beginning of humanity, but it wasn't until the mid-twentieth century that modern surgical techniques and the popularization of television brought this phenomenon into our living rooms. And thus the fascination began.

There are many sources of transgender history available, so I am not going to review that evolution in this book. But I will briefly address the changes I've seen in the ever-evolving technology and terminology of the "Sex Change Operation."

When I first started researching transgender issues in 1996, the term "sex change operation" had already fallen out of favor, and "sexual reassignment surgery" (SRS) had taken its place. By the time I came to the realization that I was truly transsexual, some surgeons were using the name "gender reassignment surgery" (GRS). There are still many other names for the surgery, but today the most commonly used terms are "gender confirmation surgery" (GCS) or "gender affirmation surgery" (GAS).

As fascinating as the media finds the alteration of one's genitals to be, the reality is, by the time a transsexual person actually has the surgical procedures done they have likely been on hormones and living as their true gender for an extended period of time. And please keep in mind there are many transgender people who, for a variety of reasons, choose not have any surgery done at all. Once again, genitals do not define gender.

By the time I had my GCS done, I had been living as Alexus full-time for two years, had been taking hormones for almost three years, and had already legally changed my name and gender. So for me, the surgery was simply the icing on the cake. Had I not told my friends and family and made a public announcement on my website, nobody except my sexual partner would have ever known.

By the time I made my decision to fully transition and have GCS, I had already been researching surgeons and talking with my transgender friends regarding different surgeons, locations, techniques, costs, etc. for a while. There are many surgeons around the world who perform a variety of different techniques, so there is more than just their reputation and bedside manner to consider. I looked at many surgical photos online and compared both the cosmetic results as well as the reported functionality. Desired post-op functionality would include things such as ease and comfort during intercourse or other sexual activities, along with the ability to climax. It has been widely reported that if you are orgasmic before GCS, you will most likely be orgasmic afterwards. And of course, with all the time, expense, and discomfort involved in the surgery, you certainly want to look and function just like any other woman when it's all over.

After months of deliberation, I chose Dr. Pierre Brassard in Montreal, Canada. At the time, the exchange rate between the US and Canada highly favored the American dollar, so that was also a financial bonus.

Sometime around mid-2000 I called Dr. Brassard's office and started the process of making an appointment. They needed the two requisite letters from my therapists recommending gender confirmation surgery, as well as a significant deposit.

Unfortunately, due to Dr. Brassard's popularity within the transgender community—combined with his already successful and busy plastic surgery practice—the next available appointment was over a year away. Still, I went ahead and made the appointment, and the date was set for October 25, 2001.

Since the wait time for my surgery was so significant, I kept myself busy with all the legalities that go along with transition. It's absolutely amazing how many places you have your name and gender recorded. But besides dealing with those logistics, I simply continued to live my life as the authentic woman I'd always been on the inside until my appointment.

Just six weeks before my scheduled surgery in Montreal, 9/11 happened, changing airport security procedures forever. I was quite concerned that I might not be able to get to Montreal for my appointment, even though I had already purchased my airline tickets—but fortunately, by the time I needed to fly to Montreal, the airports were back to the new, albeit much higher security, "normal." And since I had already changed all my legal documentation and US passport, my international flight check-in and trip through customs was uneventful.

When I arrived in Montreal, a chauffeur driving a Lincoln Town Car, sent by Dr. Brassard's office, took me to the intake and recovery convalescent facility. This was a large multi-level, multi-room facility with semi-private rooms dedicated exclusively to transgender patients who were being prepared for, or recovering from, whatever surgical procedure they were having done. It was staffed 24/7 by medical personnel, and meals were provided family style in a common dining room. So it was a great place to meet, converse, and share notes with a large variety of transgender men and women. While I was there, I would estimate that there were probably twelve to fifteen other patients in various stages of evaluation and/or recovery staying at the facility. Of course, that number changed from day to day as people came and went.

The vast majority of the patients there were M2F transgender women having GCS along with other auxiliary procedures, such as breast augmentation, rhinoplasty, and more. The age range was significant, with the youngest patient being eighteen years old and the oldest being eighty-three. The octogenarian was absolutely thrilled that she was finally getting the surgery she had wanted for so many decades, and she was an absolute delight—upbeat, energetic, active, conversant, and simply an inspiration to all who got to know her.

The eighteen-year-old had been on puberty-blocking hormones and estrogen since her pre-teen years, so she seemed like any other teenage girl. There were absolutely no external physical characteristics that would indicate she had been assigned male at birth. Fortunately, her life from this point forward would be virtually identical to any other cisgender female's.

There were also a couple F2M men at the facility who were in different stages of their transition. It was nice to chat with them and compare notes on our lives and transitions. Unlike M2F women, who typically can complete their transition in two to three procedures, F2M men often have to undergo five or more different procedures to complete their process. These procedures can include a double mastectomy, complete hysterectomy, phalloplasty, creation of a scrotum, and implantation of silicone testes. As a result of these additional procedures, it usually takes much longer, and of course is much more expensive. Partly for this reason, many trans men choose to have only the top surgery, and may or may not elect to have the bottom surgeries.

* * *

At the time I had my surgery, the private hospital where the surgeries were actually performed was a few miles away from the convalescent house. (I understand that has since changed and they are now adjacent.) As a result, I was at the convalescent house for about a day and a half prior to my surgery. This time was for orientation regarding the overall flow of things, such as timing on the day of my surgery, transportation to/from the hospital, what the pre-surgical enema entailed, and so on. I also met with Dr. Brassard during this time for pre-operative questions and a review of my health history and list of medications.

On my second night at the convalescent house, a group of four of us were taken to the hospital for check-in and pre-surgical preparation. We were all to have our surgeries the following day, two in the morning and two in the afternoon. We were placed in adjacent semi-private rooms, which had moveable room dividers for visual privacy, and told that we would be in the hospital for four days.

People often ask if I was nervous or frightened about my surgery. Nothing could have been further from the truth. I was about as excited as a child on Christmas morning. A few of the women I befriended there had some pre-operative trepidation—a quite normal reaction, given that they were about to undergo major surgery. This is, after all, a significant procedure, and it should not be taken lightly. But for many, it is also the gateway to freedom and the end of a very long transition, and for me the excitement far outweighed any nervousness I may have felt.

As I've mentioned in previous chapters, my transgender journey has also been a spiritual journey. Prior to leaving Colorado, I called the practitioner in charge of the prayer tree in our church. When I explained the procedure I was having done and told her the exact date and time of the surgery, I told her I'd like prayers for minimal pain during recovery.

"But why would you want any pain at all?" she asked, seeming surprised.

I was a bit taken aback by her question, as I simply couldn't imagine a major surgical procedure without some discomfort. She told me that assumption was my limiting belief and she'd pray for absolutely *no* pain at all. I didn't argue with her, although this seemed quite impossible to me at the time, since after my previous feminization surgery, I'd experienced a great deal of pain.

My surgery was scheduled for ten thirty in the morning—but there were some minor complications with the surgery before mine, so I wasn't actually rolled into the operating room until almost noon. When they did finally bring me into the OR, they moved me from the gurney onto the operating table and then repositioned for the procedure.

To say I was placed in an exposed, open-legged and compromised position would be an understatement. I felt as if my genitals were on the front page of *The New York Times*. But soon they placed the surgical drapes around me and I felt a bit less naked.

Once they had me situated, the anesthesiologist had me start counting backwards from one hundred, and I think I got all the way to ninety-six before finally losing consciousness.

When I awoke, I was back in my room. It seemed as if only a few seconds had passed since the anesthesiologist had last spoken to me. I actually had the thought that nothing had been done. Maybe the electricity had gone out and my procedure had been canceled? I was disappointed by the thought of that possibility, yet I was alert and had no discomfort.

I lifted the blankets to see if there were surgical bandages. The bandages were indeed there, but again, I felt no discomfort. I was simply relieved and quite happy that this final step in my transitional journey was at last complete.

The nurse came into the room a few minutes later, reassured me that the procedure had gone smoothly, and asked me if I was in any pain. She seemed surprised when I told her "no," but she went on about her business and said she'd be back in an hour or so. At that point I was able to go back to sleep and didn't wake up for another few hours.

When I awoke again, my roommate was also awake, so we compared notes. She had gotten GCS, as I had, but also breast implants and a rhinoplasty. She was in a great deal of pain and was having a difficult time speaking since her nose was completely packed with gauze and covered with surgical tape. She reminded me of how I had felt when I had my feminization surgery done in Denver a couple years prior, and I felt truly fortunate that I'd never needed a rhinoplasty or breast augmentation.

The nurse came in and gave my roommate some morphine, and she want back to sleep. Then the nurse asked me how I was feeling, and I told her I was still fine. Again, she seemed surprised.

There were no televisions in the room and I hadn't brought a book, so I was beginning to get bored. I tried to go back to sleep but my roommate was beginning to snore; not just a quiet, minor snore, but the kind of snore that sounds like a freight train whistling for the right of way. After all, she could hardly breathe with all that surgical gauze packed into her nose, and the morphine had taken her into a very deep sleep.

The nurse came back in a couple hours later and asked how I was doing. I told her a little white lie and said I was beginning to feel some significant discomfort. In reality, I just wanted her to give me something to help me go to sleep. Luckily, she didn't question my motives; she just gave me some morphine too, and off to sleep I went. What a wonderful way to pass the time . . .

The next morning we were told we would be getting out of bed and moving around a bit. That seemed a bit premature to me, but apparently that's the normal protocol. I still wasn't having any significant discomfort from the surgery, but I was stiff and sore from lying in bed for so long. With some assistance from the nurse, I hung my legs off the side of the bed. Then we managed to get me standing, and I walked a few steps in a small circle next to my bed. It felt good to move, but I soon began to get a little light-headed—after all, I'd just had a major surgical procedure, and I'd been in bed for over twenty-four hours at this point. So back into bed I went. That was the end of my exercise for post-op day one.

I continued to feign discomfort to the nurse in order to get more pain meds to help me sleep, as my roommate's snoring continued unabated.

The second day post-op we were again up and walking around a bit more. I was feeling even better now, and was able to move out into the hallway for a little more exercise. I said hello to the ladies in the adjacent room, and then I walked down to the nurses' station. Everyone seemed surprised to see me moving so easily, and I must admit, it felt good.

Day three post-op was more of the same, only this time I walked down the hall and around the corner and made a big loop on the hospital floor. Of course, all this walking was being done with a rolling IV stand that was still attached to my arm and was holding the urine bag from my catheter, which had been put in place during surgery. So it was a cumbersome walk at best.

On day four we were taken back to the convalescent home where we would stay for the remainder of our recovery. As we moved from the hospital to the cars, and then again from the cars to the convalescent home, it became apparent that I was moving around much more easily than were the other women.

Back at the convalescent home, we were assigned different roommates than we'd had in the hospital (thank goodness). This time I was assigned a very nice younger woman, in her twenties, as my roommate. Again, we were in semi-private rooms. These rooms, however, were significantly larger, so they didn't feel as industrial and sterile as the hospital rooms had. We would remain in these rooms throughout the remainder of our stay. The bathrooms were out in the hallway, as multiple rooms shared a single bath. But since most of us still had urinary catheters and had not yet had a postoperative bowel movement, the bathrooms were not in high demand.

Unlike most of the other women, my pain was still quite manageable with the help of relatively mild analgesics. However, we were about to move into a realm that none of us had ever ventured into before—one that, we were told, might be quite uncomfortable at the beginning. We were about to have our catheters and surgical dressings removed, and we were also going to start dilating multiple times a day.

Dilation is necessary to keep the new vagina (neovagina) open and functional. In essence, the surgeon has created a space where there was not one previously, and since all the surrounding tissues have not yet had time to permanently readjust to this new arrangement, it would be quite easy for things to simply collapse back to the original position. To prevent this from happening immediately after surgery, the surgeon had placed a surgical stent into my neovagina—essentially a condom filled with sterile surgical gauze—and then covered the entire site with additional surgical dressings. This temporary status quo of not having to deal with the new plumbing was about to change dramatically.

The next morning, then, was a milestone. While we were all excited about seeing our new genitals for the very first time, we were all nervous about how the stent and catheter removal would feel. We had just undergone major surgery, and now things were about to be moved around more than just a little bit. For me, this appointment created more anxiety than the actual surgery had. After all, I'd been asleep for the surgery.

The catheter came out with minimal discomfort, as it turned out, and it was an immediate relief to be free of the urine bag and IV stand. As the remaining surgical dressings were removed, the swelling and sutures immediately became apparent, but the pain was still tolerable. I must admit, I was a bit disappointed with the overall appearance of my new vulva, due to the dramatic swelling and sutures. But I was also aware from my previous feminization surgery that as the swelling subsided and the sutures were removed, things would slowly begin to appear much more normal.

Then came the removal of the surgical stent. Amazingly enough, even though it was significantly uncomfortable, it was nothing like I had imagined. This was yet another life circumstance where the imagination had created needless anxiety. The dressings were off, the catheter was gone, the surgical stent had been removed, and I was still alive and well. And best of all, there was a vulva and vagina where a penis and scrotum had been just a few days before. *Yippee!*

After cleaning the sutures and surgical area, a nurse instructed me on my first dilation. The dilators are essentially hard plastic dildos. They come in different diameters but are all the same length, and each one is marked at the appropriate depth as was determined at the time of surgery.

The procedure starts with the insertion of the smallest-diameter dilator to the requisite depth. This is almost always slightly uncomfortable; if it's not, you are probably not pushing it in far enough. You leave the dilator in place for about fifteen to twenty minutes, and then you go up to the next larger size, again to the appropriate depth. As I recall, we only used the first two or three sizes at the beginning. This was done for a total of forty-five minutes and was to be done four times a day. As a result, your day is pretty much dictated by the dilation schedule, and this continues for the entire first month post-surgery, even after returning home. After that, even though the frequency of dilation gradually decreases over time, regular dilation is a routine necessity for the rest of a transsexual woman's life. Otherwise, the depth and width of the neovagina will gradually diminish.

At this point, since the IV stands were gone and walking was much easier, walking around the convalescent house and surrounding grounds was encouraged. As I mentioned previously, it was a multilevel house; it had a basement, main floor, and upper level. This gave me my first opportunity to attempt climbing stairs, which went pretty well. In fact, one of the other women who had her surgery within days of mine commented, "You didn't have the same surgery as I did, or you wouldn't be running up and down the stairs like that!" Perhaps this was a bit of an overexaggeration, but it again showed that I was not having as much discomfort as many of the others.

Mealtime continued to give me a chance to compare notes with people who'd had surgery both before and after me. The thing that struck me as most disappointing at mealtime was the overall energy of the conversations. I expected the energy to be that of a group of transgender women and men from all different walks of life excited to be sharing a common experience. Instead, it felt like mealtime at a men's football camp. The topics were masculine, the voices masculine, and the energy was far removed from my preconceived expectation of being surrounded by a diverse group of transsexual people. I am aware that developing a feminine voice takes a great deal of practice and is quite difficult for some. But this issue is not simply about just speaking with a male voice. It goes much further than that.

While it is true that men typically have deeper voices than women, the difference is much more complex than just tone. When measured across a large sampling of people, men's voices are, on average, only three musical notes lower than women. But men tend to speak with their voice coming from deep down in their chest, whereas women have voices that resonate mostly from the neck up. Men also tend to speak in very short phrases, while women tend to be more effusive and descriptive. Men seldom speak about their feelings; women are more likely to interject feelings and perceptions into conversation. Men tend to be quite direct and use minimal wordage; women's phraseology tends to be more lyrical and descriptive. Men usually use words that are more singular; women tend to use words that are more inclusive. Men tend to end a sentence with a flat or lowered tone; women tend to lift the final word, almost as if every sentence were a question. (Please keep in mind that these descriptions are very broad generalizations, and there is much crossover in a significant percentage of either gender.)

I also realize that a broad range of characteristics is present in both men and women that are typically labeled masculine or feminine. There are strong, alpha-type women and there are energetically soft men, and there are myriad energies in between. I have conversed at length with my cisgender lesbian wife about this exact issue, and we have discovered that we are both uncomfortable with people whose overall presentation is female but with the energy of male privilege. You sometimes feel this energy at transgender conventions, where straight cisgender men are cross-dressing for the event but unfortunately neglect to check their male privilege at the front door. I absolutely did not expect to feel that energy within the group of post-op women at a surgical convalescent recovery facility.

People of privilege command their often-oversized personal space with an air of entitlement. They act as if they somehow deserve to be at the front of every line and/or sit at the head of the table. They dominate conversations and usually try to control the topic. They have an overall energy of superiority and often speak down to others, using a demeaning or belittling tone. In essence, they're simply not considerate of others' feelings, are not socially inclusive, and are generally unpleasant to be around, regardless of their gender presentation.

I realize that transition is a very individual process and there is no ultimate or universal "end result." But I believed that these individuals who were holding on to their male privilege were going to have a difficult time moving easily through society as the women they had worked so hard to become. (As I've mentioned before, Chapter 32 of this book is devoted entirely to the complex topic of passing.)

I know this will bring up significant discussion regarding the societally imposed gender binary, and it should. But we still need to address the issue of people trying to solve life issues unrelated to their gender presentation with gender reassignment surgery (the word "reassignment" used intentionally in this context). On one hand we have the World Professional Association for Transgender Health (WPATH) and the standards of care that are supposed to prevent this from happening—but on the other hand, we still have people who have reassignment surgery done for all the wrong reasons and then live to regret it.

Unfortunately, some people think all their worldly problems will be solved with gender reassignment surgery. In reality, nothing could be further from the truth. If there are social or personality issues before surgery, those issues will most certainly remain obstacles after surgery and might actually be accentuated with the additional stress of changing gender. Surgery can correct gender dysphoria and the social issues connected with living a false life, but it is not a cure-all for any other issues.

* * *

After having my catheter removed, I was concerned about my first trip to the bathroom. I wasn't sure if it would be uncomfortable or which direction the stream of urine would go in. I found that even with all the sutures, there was no discomfort, but due to the swelling, the urine was more of a spray than a stream. The other women reported similar experiences, and we were reassured that a normal stream would begin to appear as the swelling went down.

The next milestone, which is pretty much the same milestone as anyone who's had major abdominal surgery will be familiar with, is the first bowel movement. The nurses had been asking regularly about it and they had been giving us stool softener with our daily medications (nothing is secret or sacred in a facility like that one!), and finally it happened. Once again, this event turned out to be a non-event, and I was relieved in more than one sense.

Following the requisite bowel movement was our first post-surgical bath. As I mentioned earlier, the bathrooms were shared, so finding an empty bathtub was sometimes a challenge—but once we did find one, the nurses told us to take our time, sit comfortably, and relax for a while. Not only did it feel wonderful, it increased circulation to the surgical site and sped up the healing process. My first bath was the closest thing to heaven I'd felt since going in for my surgery.

Once the milestones had been checked off the list, the daily routine became just that: routine. It went something like this: wake up, dilate, have breakfast, bathe, dilate again, have lunch, walk around a bit, dilate again, have dinner, converse with other patients, dilate again, and then sleep. This process repeated itself for about ten days—and then it was finally time to return home.

★ ★ ★

One of the more interesting conversations I had while at the recovery house was with one of the F2M men. He was there for a phalloplasty (surgical creation of a penis), having already gone through the surgeries for breast removal and complete hysterectomy.

It was an interesting juxtaposition for me as a M2F woman to compare notes with an F2M man. We both wanted to be where the other person was, but at the same time we both wanted essentially the same thing: to be authentic and whole. He was most concerned about how his surgical result appeared cosmetically—primarily because he was worried about how he would appear while standing at a urinal trough. While straight cisgender men do not typically stare at other men's genitals in bathrooms, the casual glance is almost inevitable when you're standing elbow to elbow beside another urinating man, and he wondered if anyone would know that he was trans by the appearance of his penis. So he asked if I'd take a look at his new surgical result and give him my opinion.

I must admit, I was a little taken aback by his request, but at the same time I felt his genuine concern and wanted to help. So I agreed to take a look.

As he carefully unwrapped his new, delicate body part, my first response was simply, "Wow!" Not only would no one ever know he was trans, they would be completely jealous about his size. A trans man's penis is the same size both flaccid and erect. The penis is made erect by a small pump placed in the lower abdomen or scrotum, but the pump only changes the direction and rigidity of the penis; it does not make it larger as it becomes erect, as is the case in a cisgender man.

I reassured my new friend that no one would ever flinch or think, *Hey, I'll bet he's trans because of his huge penis!* I told him that he'd have a wonderful experience the first time he stood at a urinal trough, and should simply enjoy the envious glances. He was delighted with the feedback.

★ ★ ★

When it came time to fly back to Colorado after nearly two weeks in Montreal, my biggest concern was that I would be sitting in a cramped airplane seat for several hours non-stop. Fortunately, they sent us out with an inflatable rubber doughnut to help with the discomfort of sitting—and since these are fairly universally recognized as a necessity for a variety of medical conditions, I knew no one would even give it a second glance, except possibly for a look of sympathy or condolence.

I did need to get up and move around the plane a few times during the flight, but that was certainly to be expected. Otherwise the trip home went by without incident.

When I arrived home, I discovered that my youngest daughter, Erika, had decorated the entire entryway of my condo with "It's a Girl!" party banners and pink balloons. I was tearfully surprised and delighted. I love my daughters!

The next few weeks were still dominated by the dilation schedule, and as the swelling subsided, the chore slowly changed into something that was just minimally uncomfortable. It wasn't sexually arousing, but I could tell that nerve endings were being rerouted and healed, and becoming sensate. Things were beginning to appear and function as the new norm.

My partner, Cristina, seemed delighted with the new result, and as the healing progressed, we experimented with a variety of new sex toys. As predicted, it took several months before I became fully orgasmic, but it was worth the wait.

PART THREE

My Postoperative Life
(2001–Present)

"All that is valuable in human society depends upon the opportunity for development accorded the individual."
—Albert Einstein

My gender confirmation surgery on October 25, 2001 officially ended my transitional stage and marked the beginning of the rest of my life—one in which I could live authentically as the woman I had finally become.

The remaining chapters in this book will deal with a multitude of issues that affect most or all transgender people at one time or another. Some of the chapters are trans-specific issues, and others are fairly universal and may speak to cisgender women as well.

I didn't pick up writing again until two years after my surgery, primarily because I was enjoying living my new life during that time. As I mentioned in the previous chapter, I had taken my website offline prior to surgery.

But then, two years into my new life, I decided to write again—new pieces that shared my new perspective.

(2016 Note: While this introductory piece was written after my GCS in 2001, my perspective as a maturing middle-aged lesbian woman was, and still is, in a state of gradual evolution. I would like to think this evolution of perspective is a result of both maturity and wisdom.)

Chapter 19

A Retrospective on My Transition
(2003)

It has been nearly two years since my GRS and almost four years since transitioning into full-time womanhood. I want to share some new insights and encourage those still contemplating transition to do a reality check about how it might look and feel after the excitement wanes.

Being transsexual is an all-consuming condition for the years (or decades) prior to transition. Not a day goes by without that deep-down dysphoric feeling that something is wrong and/or missing in your life. Since that feeling is *so* pervasive for *so* long, it seems that simply getting rid of that feeling is reason enough to transition. And in many ways, it is enough. But the real wake-up call comes in what life feels like after the dysphoria is gone and the transition is complete. What does it feel like on "the other side"?

What it feels like for me is surprisingly similar to what my life was before my transition. I am confronted with the exact same issues that most other women in America are faced with: relationships, parenting, household chores and duties, career, paying the bills, etc. It feels very normal, and at times boring. Some of the nuances of everyday life are slightly different for me now that I'm in a same-sex relationship, but for the most part, they're not significantly different just because I lived the first forty-seven years of my life as a man.

It's only after I've known someone for an extended period of time that the topic of lesbianism or transsexuality even comes up. For some, being trans is the most important part of their identity, and they may feel the desire to bring their identity to the forefront right away. I generally wait to see what people's knowledge and/or interest level is, and wait until someone asks something about my current or past life requiring a response that, if I answer honestly, will reveal my transgender history. They might ask something like, "What did your children's father do?" At this point, I have the option to give a "stealth" answer that allows them to continue thinking I'm cisgender and the biological mother of my children, or I can answer honestly and tell them my ex was a woman and I'm actually transsexual and the biological father of my children. This split-second decision is based on intuition, and for me there are no hard and fast rules.

How I feel about a particular person generally plays into my response. Then, based on their reaction and/or interest level, a short version of "TS 101" may be necessary—a conversation that may take anywhere from a few minutes to a couple hours. Most of the time, that is the end of any discussion about something that has consumed years of my life! Sometimes that feels disappointing, but I try to keep in mind that these are my issues, and the average person is quite busy with their own life. Listening to my story is not usually very high on their list of interests.

I thought, like many pre-transition transsexuals, that once my transition was complete and my SRS was done, life would be a bed of roses and every day would be more exciting than the day before. I thought just being a woman would be enough to make life complete. For me, that simply has not been the case. Life has become routine. It is certainly not more routine than my previous life as a male dentist, but it is more "ordinary" than I expected it to be.

Let me be clear: I am *not* saying I have any regrets about transitioning. I think expressing my authentic essence literally saved my life. What I am saying is that life goes on, in a rather ordinary way, after the gender dysphoria is gone. The absence of dysphoria does not necessarily produce euphoria, although it may for a short period of time. Instead, the absence of dysphoria is "normal." And normal is whatever you make of it—good, bad, or indifferent.

So, what is the point of this rather sobering treatise? Simply this: I want to encourage any pre-transitioning readers to be realistic in their expectations. Try to take a logical and realistic look at what life will be like months or years after transition. Without this truthful and sometimes difficult look into how the post-transition life may look and feel, there can be a tendency to overexaggerate expectations and think life will be just perfect.

Just like some new mothers can experience postpartum depression after having a baby, some recent post-op transsexuals can go through a similar postoperative depressive period. Once the emotional pendulum has swung from dysphoria up to euphoria, the movement back toward normal can feel like an impending return of dysphoria. This feeling can be frightening, and at times overwhelming. Just know that it is normal, and to some degree, predictable. Normal is not the same as dysphoric.

Only when this postoperative emotional roller coaster had come to a complete and full stop did I actually feel that I had completely transitioned. At this point I had finally arrived at my ultimate destination: womanhood.

MY CURRENT PERSPECTIVE
As the writing dates of my previous pieces get closer and closer to the present day, the differences between "then and now" will become less and less noticeable.

When writing this piece, I didn't really specify what sort of overexaggerated expectations I have repeatedly seen within the post-op community. The most common "fantasy" I have observed is the belief that once transition is complete, all other issues will somehow melt away. Nothing could be further from the truth. If you are experiencing financial, psychosocial, or relationship issues preoperatively, those issues will almost certainly remain after transition is complete.

Beyond that, my thoughts on this particular subject haven't significantly changed. As the years pass, however, my memories of my pre-transition dysphoria fade further and further from my present-day life. It's difficult to comprehend that something that was so all-encompassing for me for so many long years is now simply gone—*poof!*—but that's the truth. And it truly is magical.

Those fading memories are one of the primary reasons I am writing this book. I fully realize that there are many people, in all walks of life, still living every single day in the misery that is gender dysphoria. I hope these post-transitional chapters will give hope and encouragement to those still struggling. It can get better!

Note: I am also aware that my personal experience has been greatly enhanced by the fact that in casual day-to-day living, I almost always pass as cisgender. Again, I will address this issue in greater detail in Chapter 32.

Chapter 20

My Thoughts on the BBL Controversy

Is Autogynephilia a Real Diagnosis?
(2004)

(2015 Note: Wikipedia defines Ray Blanchard's "autogynephilia transsexuality" as "the condition where men are purportedly sexually aroused at the idea of having a female body." This description completely negates transsexual women as authentic women. Instead, it reduces us to men with a paraphilic fetish of wanting a female body.)

Bailey-Blanchard-Lawrence—BBL—is a compilation of theory and transsexual taxonomy espoused over the past decade and a half by three people: J. Michael Bailey, Ray Blanchard, and Anne Lawrence. For an in-depth analysis, please visit Andrea James's Bailey-Blanchard-Lawrence clearinghouse online. She does such a marvelous job documenting this whole controversy that I do not feel the need to go into detail here. I simply want to give my thoughts on the subject.

When I first became aware of my gender identity dysphoria (GID) late in 1996, the relatively new term "autogynephilia" was just beginning to gain some usage within the transgender community. My understanding at that time was that the term was being used to describe those individuals who did not fit the "classic" definition of transsexuality. I knew it had been coined in 1989 by Ray Blanchard of the Clarke Institute in Toronto, Canada, but naively thought it was an innocent word. At that point in my life I was relatively uninformed regarding the politics of the psychological and transgender communities, so was unaware of the building controversy.

When I first heard the term, I thought it must apply to me. After all, my personal transgender history did not match many of the descriptors for classic transsexuality, and like most people struggling with GID, my self-esteem was at an all-time low. As a result, I was actively looking for any label or classification that would help me feel more hopeful and less alone. I openly declared myself to be an "autogynephilic transsexual woman," feeling that identifying as autogynephilic would lend at least some sort of credibility to my struggle.

In 1997, when I initially read Anne Lawrence's essay "Men Trapped in Men's Bodies," I was disturbed by the statement, "autogynephilia can be seen as a type of paraphilia." I knew that my gender dysphoria was not about fetishism, but also felt that because I would never be considered a "classic transsexual," I had no other choice. I labeled myself autogynephilic by default. I found some consolation in Dr. Becky Allison's rebuttal, but I still felt like some sort of second-class transsexual.

When I closed my original website late in 2000, I moved my transsexual life into relative stealth mode. I was starting a new relationship and simply enjoying my new life as a woman. I did not actively follow any transgender websites for nearly three years.

When I reentered the online community in May of 2003,

I was completely unaware of the events that had transpired during my absence.

When I began to rebuild my website, I sent a few "announcement" e-mails to some of the more visible post-op transsexual women I could find on the Web. I was using a combination of new material, along with some historically relevant old writings, in order to build my online presence quickly. In one of the descriptions of my transgender evolution, I described myself as an autogynephilic transsexual woman (knowing I still did not fit the "classic" definition of transsexual). I owe a great deal of thanks to Lynn Conway for quickly and gently telling me that I should reconsider the use of that term, making reference to the BBL controversy and Mike Bailey's book *The Man Who Would Be Queen*. When I followed her recommended links, I was shocked!

The entire BBL model of transsexuality is a complete insult to the psychological, scientific, and transgender communities. To call it any form of real science is not only fraudulent but also patently absurd. As a practicing dentist for twenty years, I am familiar with the long-established requirements and well-defined parameters any study must meet in order to be considered valid scientific research—and the "junk science" of this group, and more specifically Bailey's book, would never make it past the first phase of peer review. The book is mostly anecdotal and contains no legitimate scientific research, and if taken seriously by the psychological community, it would set the entire transgender movement back by twenty years. Luckily, I have enough confidence in the psychological community to know that will not happen.

I have no issue with how Anne Lawrence chooses to describe herself. If she considers herself an autogynephilic transsexual, using the combined definition of the BBL model, that is completely her decision. However, she does *not* have the right to include the rest of us in her (or should I say "his"?)

male paraphilic model based simply on the fact that we transitioned late in life.

As Andrea James so aptly put it, Bailey and Lawrence have it "categorically wrong." I completely agree, and of the dozens of transsexual women I know personally, not a single person fits into either of their narrow and distorted definitions.

So why do I care? As a spiritual woman who prides herself in maintaining a "live and let live" attitude, why am I even bothering to address this issue? The answer is simple: people are being *hurt* by the promotion of these self-serving, arrogant theories.

People are being hurt when Anne Lawrence serves on the board of the Harry Benjamin International Gender Dysphoria Association and claims to represent the entire transsexual community as an advocate. This claim is being made even as she actively promotes this new BBL model as the one and only "correct" classification for all transsexuals.

People are being hurt when gatekeepers in the psychological and psychiatric community begin to "restrict" rather than "expand" their definitions of transsexuality based on junk science theories like the BBL model.

People are being hurt when they are actively struggling with gender identity dysphoria and are made to feel even worse because the label of paraphilia is being forced on them by the BBL model (or, worse yet, when they are told they are *lying* about their true feelings and motivations, simply because they do not fit within these narrow and rigid parameters).

People are being hurt when Bailey's book is being promoted or accepted as real science and therefore used as a resource against us by those who are already transphobic for a multitude of societal or religious reasons. (Categorizing all late-transitioning transsexual women as paraphilic men completely and absurdly discounts our deeply held identities as women.)

People are being hurt when they begin to explore the transgender world online and are forced back into the closet of unhappiness and self-denial due to fear of being labeled "paraphilic" (as if being transsexual is not daunting enough by itself).

People are being hurt when this ridiculous subject polarizes the entire transsexual community.

I could continue to elaborate, but by now you get the idea.

It is time for all of us to speak out and be heard! Only when the multitudes of self-confident transsexual women speak out with a coherent, intelligent, and indignant voice will we truly be heard. Then, and only then, will we finally gain the collective and individual respect we so deeply deserve.

MY CURRENT PERSPECTIVE

This was a highly charged political issue when I wrote this piece back in 2003, and unfortunately, it remains so to this very day. It is beyond the scope of this book to delve deeply into the politics of transgender issues, along with the religious and societal pressures that want us to simply disappear from the face of the earth. But suffice it to say, transsexuality is not a paraphilia, and trans women are not simply men who want to wear a woman's body. That belief system is truly as absurd as it sounds.

Chapter 21

Stealth?
(2005)

When I first heard the word "stealth" (in regards to the transgender community) many years ago, I was actually in disbelief that there were many postoperative transsexuals, both M2F and F2M, living their lives as if they had never transitioned. I couldn't imagine how they could go through the psychological and physical pain and suffering that is inherent in transition, and then leave it behind as if it had never happened. Yet there was a part of me that thought such a life would be absolutely amazing. Living and being perceived by others as cisgender seemed to me, at least on the surface, to be every transsexual person's dream. But I would soon discover that this "freedom" comes at a great cost.

I knew that many decades ago it was considered quite normal to transition and then move to another state, start a new job, disconnect from all past friends and family, and start a completely new life. In fact, not only was it the norm, it was the standard protocol at the time—one that was recommended and enforced by the professionals who treated transsexuals.

But I thought times had changed . . .

Now, nearly a decade later, when I look back on my early days of transition, I can see that my primary concern was being "read" (being recognized as transgender). Therefore the goal was quite simply "passing." Living in stealth seemed absurd and impossible at first—but as time went on, the estrogen began to have its magical effect. By this point I was several months into my real-life test (RLT), another mandatory step in getting the letters required for surgery. (I was also working diligently on my voice.) By the time I had completed my RLT, had my letters for surgery, and had successfully refined my voice, what had seemed formerly impossible now didn't seem so absurd.

As my new life in the suburbs settled into normalcy, I authored my second website and Cristina and I started an online life coaching business together. As a result, I was back out in the open again—but this time in an intentional way, to reach out to those who were struggling. That site was active for about three more years.

Then the Universe began to orchestrate my next chapter in life.

Cristina and I broke up. We sold our house in the suburbs, and I bought a new condominium in another Denver suburb. I also started a new job—driving as a courier—and since I was spending most of my days alone in my car delivering packages, there was really no opportunity for me to engage in significant interpersonal interactions. But the seeds of living in stealth began to germinate. All of a sudden, I had a chance to be seen in a completely new environment where nobody knew my history.

Next came a new job offer as a corporate sales representative in Northern California—one that would require me to move away from Denver.

In no time, I found myself with a new job in a new state, in a new city, with new friends, a new boss, new connections, etc. . . . and guess what? I slipped easily and quickly into complete stealth.

Suddenly I understood the true meaning behind the word. I took my website down and sent requests to everyone who had formerly linked to my page to remove their links. Everyone was quite respectful, but I could also tell there were a few who were judging my decision to once again move into stealth (the first time being several years before, when I first moved out to the Denver suburbs with Cristina).

At this point, I think it is relevant to describe the behaviors I consider to be emblematic of "living in stealth," all of which I adapted upon moving to California. To paraphrase Bree from the movie *Transamerica*, "It isn't necessary to go around blabbing my entire medical history to anyone who will listen."

It's easy to fall into stealth behavior, even among people who are in my circle of close and intimate friends. Leading people to think I am my daughters' biological mother is stealth. Letting people think my ex-spouse was a man is stealth. Leading people to believe I grew up on a farm as a "tomboy" is stealth. Essentially this was about passing as cisgender, and in some situations heterosexual. Even though I had dabbled with living in stealth while living in Denver, I moved completely into stealth when I moved to California—and though it seemed like the easier thing to do in the moment, I soon discovered that living in stealth also came at a price.

For me, that cost was my integrity. There was the nagging and nearly constant feeling that the half-truths and deception around my childhood, former marriage, and children were taking away from the joy of living a cheerful and authentic current life. And there was the ever-present concern regarding what would happen if someone discovered my past and I got "outed" at work or socially.

I had spent years trying to prove to the world who I truly *am*, but along the way I had lost the foundational piece of who I *was*. We are a combination of our past lives, our present experiences, and our future dreams. Without all the pieces, I felt like I had an incomplete life. I had come too far to stop now.

Another cost of living in stealth is the damage it does to our transgender community. How is society ever going to learn and change if we hide ourselves from view? I have always been open about being a lesbian, but since there is more prejudice and discrimination against transsexuality, I often took the easy way out. I have readily affirmed my life as a lesbian but often omitted an essential truth. Lying by omission is as harmful as lying by commission—and in this case, the hurt always comes back to me.

As I became increasingly aware of the personal cost of living without integrity, I started to contemplate coming out of stealth. For me, the precipitating event was my viewing of the wonderful Logo documentary movie, *Beautiful Daughters*. It is readily available from multiple sources online; if you haven't seen it already, it is an absolute must! The film highlights the courage of several of my personal heroines: Lynn Conway, Andrea James, Calpernia Addams, Leslie Townsend, and many other courageous transsexual women. Seeing those women interview, rehearse, and perform in the all-transgender 2004 production of *The Vagina Monologues* was truly inspirational. It was the precipitating event for this writing and the re-creation of my website.

I am not saying there is never a time or place to live in stealth. Quite the contrary! There are many situations in which living is stealth is not only convenient, it is essential for survival. The potential economic impact of being fired for being transgender is a legitimate concern for many. And there are the all-too-real physical dangers that can arise from coming out to the wrong person. Only on an individual, case-by-case basis can someone decide when—or *if*—to come out of stealth. Nobody can, or should, decide for you.

I can only state what is currently in my heart.

I am resolved to stop living in stealth, committed to being proud of the woman I have become, and am finally standing strong in the entirety of my truth!

MY CURRENT PERSPECTIVE
Other than in casual interactions with the relative strangers I encounter in everyday living and/or at the random social event, I no longer live my life at any level of intentional stealth. I am completely open and out as a transgender woman. But this level of being out does not mean that I intentionally tell every person to whom I'm introduced that I am transsexual. There is a fine line between being openly out and being socially or conversationally inappropriate.

The decision about whether or not to inform a relatively new acquaintance about my medical history is made on a case-by-case basis. There are no hard-and-fast rules. It depends on how we were introduced, whether we have friends in common, and how much I know about their beliefs and/or politics. Some people are energetically open and the conversation goes fairly deep pretty quickly. These are the people who feel like instantaneous old friends. Typically, they are invited into my inner circle of confidential conversation very quickly, sometimes in our very first conversation. On the other hand, there are some new friends with whom I never reach that level of intimate conversation. Every conversation seems very light and only surface topics are discussed. I may not ever disclose my past to those people, as it would seem inappropriate and serve no purpose.

Then, of course, there are the acquaintances who fall somewhere in the middle. I'm fairly good at asking questions that will allow people to tell me who they are, if they are open to sharing personal details about their lives. For that group, their level of sharing will determine when my past might become relevant to our exchange of personal detail.

Once again, it's always case by case.

I also didn't mention in this piece that after about a year and a half in my new job, I was outed by a curious and Internet-savvy coworker. (Nothing can ever be completely removed from the Internet.) Fortunately for me, being outed was essentially a non-event. Since I was already an extremely successful saleswoman in my new position—number two in the entire country, to be exact—my boss couldn't have cared less about my medical history. So that news filtered quickly through the company but disappeared almost as fast as it came.

I fully recognize that I was one of the lucky ones. For many transgender people, being outed at work can be grounds for immediate dismissal. As of the time of this writing, you can still be fired for being transgender in thirty-one states. This is just one example of the types of bias many transgender people face every day. Fortunately, there is slow, gradual progress being made toward ending this blatant discrimination as progressive businesses, cities, counties, and various other public entities are adding transgender protection to their non-discrimination clauses.

Chapter 22

How We Met and Our Brief Courtship
(2006)

Strangely enough, this is another significant life event about which I never really wrote at length on my website. Once again, as my new life began to unfold, I was quite happy just "being" and didn't take the time to sit down and write an extended description of either my courtship, engagement, or beautiful wedding day with Deb. As a result, these next three chapters are written from my current perspective (in 2015) with a few short written descriptions from 2006–2007.

* * *

When I first moved to San Jose in the fall of 2005, I was initially entirely consumed by the process of learning the techniques and nuances of my new job. It was a 100 percent commissioned sales position as a regional manager for a corporate communications company based out of Connecticut. So if I didn't sell, I didn't get paid.

The move was made easier by the fact that I was now single. Cristina and I had ended our five-year relationship about a year earlier, so I was now quite comfortable with being a single woman. After that breakup, I made a conscious decision not to date for at least a year so I could learn at a deep, personal level who I had become and live my new life as a single, middle-aged woman, outside of any sort of relationship.

After the first few months of learning my job, and after having some success with my first few sales, I decided to explore the LGBT social scene in downtown San Jose and the nearby suburbs. San Jose is the third-largest city in California and has a very vibrant downtown area full of restaurants, theaters, and nightclubs. So there was never a shortage of activities that could keep me distracted. But I was now beginning to seek significant friendships and was looking for a group of people to whom I could relate—people I could simply hang out with.

There were a couple of interesting places in the downtown area, but since San Jose State University was also downtown, most of the local bars and restaurants were frequented by a crowd of much younger people. So I started expanding my social horizons to the suburbs.

I found a nice lesbian club in Sunnyvale, but the majority of women I saw there were closer to my daughters' age group than mine. There was another gay bar in nearby Mountain

View, but most of the regulars were men. I knew there had to be a neighborhood hangout for middle-aged lesbian women somewhere in Silicon Valley!

I finally found what I was looking for out in Cupertino. Dar's was located in a small, nondescript strip mall on the west side of the San Jose metro area, and it was named after the friendly woman who owned the place.

I was a bit nervous the first time I went in, but Dar took it upon herself not only to introduce herself to every new customer that came through her door but to walk them around the bar after their first drink and introduce them to everyone else in the place. As a result, I was only a stranger for about five minutes. I knew instantly that I had found my new neighborhood hangout, even though it was a twenty-minute drive from my downtown apartment.

Since I didn't know anyone else in downtown San Jose, Dar's became my home away from home when I wasn't either on the road selling corporate communication systems or working from my downtown apartment making cold calls and organizing my ongoing appointments. After a few visits to Dar's, when I walked in, it was very much like *Cheers*—everybody knew my name. I became one of the regulars, as Dar's was my only real distraction from work. It was there that I met many other women who I could go hiking or to a movie with, or just hang out with at their house for a casual dinner and drinks.

This was most definitely a lesbian bar, and I had never seen another trans woman there. There were a few gay men that occasionally came through, but for the most part it was a women's hangout. Unlike many of the "lesbian bars" you see in movies or on television, there were no high-femme lipstick lesbians wearing stiletto heels and looking like they just stepped off a fashion show runway. These were regular women, wearing regular clothes and living regular lives. The spectrum typically ran from butch to soft butch to soft femme. But it was fairly unusual to see anyone wearing a skirt or dress, unless they were coming from another party or special event. Dar's was simply a comfortable neighborhood women's bar.

All of us regulars sat at the far end of the bar, away from the front door. That location gave us the best overall view of the entire place and was least disturbed by people coming in and going out. It also gave us easy access to the jukebox, restrooms, and karaoke corner.

On a typical karaoke Friday night in February of 2006, my friends and I were at our usual spot at the bar when Dar came over to give us a heads up about someone new in the bar. She pointed to an attractive, dark-haired woman in a deep green business suit who was already introducing herself to the people seated around her. She had a big, radiant smile that was absolutely captivating. Dar informed us that her name was Deb. I knew from past experience that Dar would soon be introducing her to everyone in the bar, so I waited for her to make her rounds.

Since it was karaoke night, people were moving around to and from our end of the bar as they sang their songs and mingled with other tables throughout the area and near the stage. As a result, I had the opportunity to make certain there was an empty barstool immediately to my right.

As expected, in just a few minutes' time, Dar brought Deb down to our group and began the introductions. Once again, Deb flashed her big, beautiful smile, and she looked each individual person in the eyes as she shook their hand. As I shook her hand, I was immediately stunned by her strong yet soft energy and asked her if she'd like to sit in the empty seat that just "happened" to be on my right. She accepted my invitation and we began to talk.

We started with the usual small talk about what we did for a living. She was the Senior Vice President of Organizational Transformation for an Internet company in nearby Santa Clara. When I confessed I didn't know what that meant, she explained, "Essentially, my job is to keep everyone in the organization on the same page."

When she asked about my job I said, "I sell communications systems to forward-thinking companies that want to keep everyone in their organization on the same page." She looked at me and raised her eyebrows, and I returned her surprised look; it was as if both of us were saying, "Is this for real?" Not only did we have something in common regarding our businesses, for me, there was already an underlying personal interest developing. Deb was obviously intelligent, articulate, extroverted, and personable. I was instantly attracted. To me, the sexiest part of a person is their brain.

Since it was a Friday night and the workweek was supposedly over, we exchanged business cards and agreed that I should come to her office early the following week so I could do a formal presentation for her and her entire team. Then we could discuss how we might do business together. That achieved, we mutually agreed that the rest of the night should be for meeting people and having fun. No more shop talk!

The next few hours flew by as we discussed just about everything else imaginable. It was truly one of those conversations where you feel like you've known someone for a very long time, even though you just met. I also sang a couple of karaoke songs to keep the evening fun and light.

Shortly after midnight, Deb said she needed to head home, as she lived about forty-five minutes away in a Silicon Valley bedroom community called Pleasanton. I thought I should walk her out to her car to be polite and say good night.

As we stepped out the front door, I immediately saw an unfamiliar car in the parking lot: a white Mercedes Benz 500 SL hardtop convertible parked in the corner spot near the street. Without thinking, I asked, "Is that your car?"

I immediately felt like a socially awkward high school girl and was embarrassed by my question; it seemed so silly and superficial after the deep conversation we'd been having all night. But Deb seemed unfazed and answered, "Yes, it is!"—and once again, she flashed that big, beautiful smile in my direction. I figured at this point I might as well continue with my inadvertent performance as the inappropriate teenager and asked, "Can I touch it?"

We both laughed as we walked over to her car and she opened the driver's side door. As I sat down in the plush leather seat and put my hands on the smooth, glossy, burled wood steering wheel, Deb simply stood back and continued to smile at me.

After a few moments of automotive admiration, I got out of the car, told her how much I'd enjoyed the evening, and asked, "So, are you going to call me or am I going to call you?"

Deb, being the take-charge woman she is, said, "I'll call you Monday morning."

I walked away with the feeling that something inside me was stirring. This was a butterflies-in-the-stomach kind of feeling that I hadn't felt for anyone in well over a year. I was most definitely interested in her, and I hoped she felt the same about me.

★ ★ ★

Over the weekend I spent a great deal of time contemplating when and if I would tell Deb that I was transgender. I knew we were likely to do business together, but I also had feelings for her already. This consumed a fair amount of my headspace as I eagerly awaited her call.

She called Monday morning, as promised, to schedule an appointment for my formal presentation. This presentation would demonstrate the communication system I had briefly told her about and recommended at our first meeting at Dar's. The next mutually available time slot was in two days, late Wednesday afternoon, so we made the appointment for 4 p.m.

She then asked if that would be my last appointment of the day, and if so, if I would like to join her for dinner afterwards. My intuition had been correct—she was interested in getting to know me on a personal level, too.

Since this had the potential to be my first significant relationship in over a year and a half, I was nervous. On the one hand, I didn't want to tell her too early about being transsexual; but if I waited too long, she might feel deceived, or even worse, lied to. It felt like a "damned if you do, damned if you don't" situation.

After weighing my options, I made the decision to simply move forward with the business presentation and then see how it felt when we went to dinner afterwards.

* * *

When Wednesday afternoon arrived, I made sure to dress a little nicer than my usual day-to-day business attire. I didn't go overboard with anything too formal; I just wanted to be certain that I looked as professional as possible.

When I arrived at the corporate headquarters where Deb worked, I checked in with the receptionist, got a security badge, and then waited for Deb to come to the lobby. When she arrived at the top of the stairway leading down to the lobby, she once again flashed that smile of hers and invited me up to the second floor, where she escorted me to the conference room.

The presentation went well. Deb let me know that she and her staff would discuss my proposal amongst themselves over the next couple days and we'd talk again very soon. The meeting was dismissed, and just as planned, it was then quitting time.

Deb and I walked out of her office building and into the employee parking lot. She said she'd be happy to drive us to dinner at a restaurant nearby, and I could leave my car in the visitors' parking area. Since I was finished with my "business professional" persona for the day, I accepted her offer to drive and got into her car. In my mind, we had entered into the "date" mode.

She took me to an upscale restaurant inside the nearby Marriott Hotel—where, she said, she often entertained business clients. She valet parked the car and we went into the adjacent restaurant. Since she was somewhat of a regular there, the staff all knew her by name; they warmly welcomed us and seated us at a relatively private booth. Now it was *really* beginning to feel like a date.

By now I was getting nervous and I was feeling ready to tell her about my history. I was already confident that my personal story wasn't going to affect our business relationship, and I wanted to start our personal relationship with a foundation of complete honesty. At the same time, however, it seemed too early in the evening for such a significant conversation. I was torn between being completely honest about my past, because it seemed like the right thing to do, and being afraid that she might reject me as "not a real woman." Unfortunately, this is a feeling quite common to many (if not most) trans women when starting a new relationship.

As soon as we were seated our server came over, explained the specials for the day, gave us both menus, and handed Deb the wine list. Since moving to California, I had been familiarizing myself with some of the wonderful local wines but really didn't yet know how to choose between a good wine and a great wine. So I asked Deb what she was thinking as she browsed through the multi-page wine list. She asked me if I preferred red or white and if I had any idea about what entrée I might order. I told her I hadn't yet decided what I was going to order but wanted her recommendation for a wine that was red, robust, and not too dry. She chose one that was about three times more expensive than anything I had ever ordered before, so at this point the date had elevated to the next level of elegance.

When the wine came, Deb ordered a couple of appetizers, and then she proposed a toast. We toasted to success in business, great new friendships, and an adventurous life. By now I was so nervous that my heart felt like it was about to pound out of my chest. The time to have *the* serious conversation had arrived. Although I had told myself I would wait until evening progressed before sharing my past, the level of intimacy in our conversation had already reached a level where *not* telling her would feel dishonest. I was feeling out of integrity and needed to say something.

I took a couple sips of my wine and said, "Because it feels like our new friendship has moved very quickly into something more significant, I have something I need to tell you." I paused, took a deep breath, and said, "I lived the first forty-five years of my life as a man."

Her response took the form of a question: "Are you still in touch with your family?"

Certainly not the response I expected. "Yes," I said. "It was a little rough on my parents for a few years, but we've since moved past it and are now quite close again."

I then told her I fully transitioned in 2001 and started to give more detail about how long I'd known I was trans, when I started my transition, etc.—but Deb interrupted me and said, "I'm really not interested in hearing your medical history. I am interested in knowing who you are today. That's really all that matters." Then she asked me what I wanted for dinner.

Needless to say, I was dumbfounded and elated at the same time. I was both relieved at her immediate acceptance and a little disappointed that she didn't seem to want any more details. You could have knocked me out of the booth with a feather.

As the evening went on we had a wonderful meal, great wine, and fantastic conversation. Later in the evening, I couldn't help but ask her if she'd already figured out that I was transgender the first night we met at Dar's. She said she had some suspicions a couple of times throughout the evening, but since she was interested in me as a person, it hadn't really mattered. She said she had asked herself, "Are you ready for this?" and the answer was yes. Otherwise, there was no significant conversation about my being trans.

Once again, I was dumbfounded. I had never met someone so unconditionally loving.

As we drove back to my car, Deb asked me if she could see me again. When I said, "Of course," she asked if I had any plans for Friday night. After telling her that I did not, she said she'd make all the arrangements for that evening but for now to plan on going to dinner and then out for some other evening event afterwards. We agreed that she would pick me up at six for our first official date.

By that time I had moved from my apartment in downtown San Jose to an extended-stay corporate hotel at the extreme southeast edge of the city. Since I drove to all my appointments, and since my territory went for many miles in all directions, it didn't really matter to me where I lived in the San Jose metropolitan area. I had chosen the hotel based on easy access to multiple freeways, a fast Internet connection, and reasonable monthly pricing. But coming from where Deb lived, it was definitely on the far side of town.

* * *

On Friday, Deb picked me up promptly at six and we started to drive north through San Jose.

She asked me if I'd been to San Francisco since moving to the Bay Area, and I told her I'd been there only for business meetings, and most of those were around the airport. She asked me if I'd ever heard of *Beach Blanket Babylon*. I hadn't, so she explained to me that it was the world's longest-running musical revue, and was a pop-culture spoof following Snow White through many social and political scenarios in San Francisco and throughout the United States. It sounded great to me. So we had another nice dinner at a restaurant close to the venue, and then we walked to the show. On the way there, Deb asked if she could hold my hand as we walked.

After the show, we had a drink at a nearby bar and then started the drive back to my hotel. The drive from the show took over an hour, so by the time we got there, we were both tired. And poor Deb still had another forty-five-minute drive from my hotel back to her house in Pleasanton. I felt so sorry for her; this one single date had required her to drive for nearly four hours. I thought to myself, *She must be in love.* I knew I was certainly beginning to feel that way, and I hoped the feeling was mutual.

We continued to see each other two or three times a week from that point on, and I tried to coordinate my drives to and from my appointments with her work schedule so we could have a dinner date without an absurd amount of driving for either of us. But as Deb is quite the traditionalist when it comes to dating and relationships, on the weekend she would absolutely insist that she come to my hotel and pick me up so we could go out for an official date. As a result, she was keeping some very late hours.

About two weeks into our relationship, Deb called me with a proposition. She said she was not yet ready to have sex, but would like to spend an entire weekend together. Since she lived in a three-bedroom, two-bath house, she wanted me to drive to Pleasanton, go out with her on a date there, and then spend the night in one of the guest bedrooms. That way we could stay out late, sleep in the next morning, and then have a leisurely brunch someplace nearby. Since there were no expectations for anything physical, we could both relax and simply enjoy each other's company. What a great way to get to know each other even better.

The following weekend we repeated the same scenario, but this time we didn't sleep in separate bedrooms.

Shortly after our second weekend together, as it was apparent to both of us that our relationship was rapidly maturing, Deb suggested that I move out of my hotel and in with her. Even though it seemed rather quick to me, it also felt "just right," and completely appropriate for two fifty-something lesbians.

Just over three weeks after the day we met, I rented a U-Haul and moved into Deb's house. So we were a little slow compared to the old joke about lesbians bringing a U-Haul to their second date—but not too far behind!

★ ★ ★

After moving in with Deb, I was constantly overwhelmed with her generosity. She showered me with gifts, took me out on dates at least twice a week, and shared absolutely everything with me.

Only about a week after I moved in, she started asking me when we were going to get married. I kept telling her it was simply too early. After all, we'd only known each other for a few weeks. With that as my only response, she would simply smile and say, "I love you and I want to spend the rest of my life with you. What are you waiting for?"

I didn't really have an answer to that question. So every few days, she'd ask again, and every time, my answer would always the same. It just felt too fast, and although it may sound a bit cliché, it all seemed too good to be true.

We were already getting out of the house and going on official dates consistently, but one day Deb came home with a package and said she had a present for me. When I opened it, I found a nice piece of carry-on, weekender-style luggage. When I looked at her quizzically, she said that not only did she want to travel the world with me, she wanted me to travel in style.

And until we could make some bigger plans, she first wanted to take me to a nice hotel in Monterey—a beautiful seaside community on the Pacific coast about two hours south of where we were living—for a long weekend. So we planned on going the very next weekend.

By this time, we had been living together for less than a month and my head was still spinning with all her generosity. She had completely opened up her house to me and insisted on paying for everything. I offered to pay some rent, buy groceries, pay the utilities, or help out financially in some way, but she simply refused all my offers to share expenses.

Even though we were both still working and were therefore quite busy, the quality time we spent together was so warm and unconditionally loving, it felt as if we'd already been a couple for a very long time. My feelings for her had quickly moved from the early relationship "puppy love" into a deep and significant "I think I could live with this woman forever" kind of love. Apparently that's what can happen when you fall in love in your fifties. So, unbeknownst to Deb, I decided to accept her proposal for marriage when we were in Monterey.

We stayed in a beautiful hotel right on the water, had a wonderful massage in the hotel spa, and then went to a really nice restaurant for drinks and dinner. Our server was a very sweet young woman, and about halfway through our dinner she asked how many years we'd been a couple. We told her we'd only met about a month previous and she seemed shocked. She said we had the energy of a couple that had been together for many years. Interestingly enough, we'd recently been told the exact same thing at another party we attended.

After dinner, we took a leisurely walk past the shops on Cannery Row and happened into a nice jewelry store. The lady behind the counter, a complete stranger to both of us, greeted us with the question, "Are you ladies here to pick out an engagement ring?" I glibly answered, "Apparently so!" We all laughed and we looked at some nice rings but didn't actually pick anything out.

As we left the jewelry store and began to walk down the street again, I said to Debbie, "You know that question that you keep asking me? Well, the answer is yes." She seemed absolutely thrilled to hear those words, gave me a great big kiss, and said, "We're going to have the best wedding ever!" So we were officially engaged. And even though it just happened to be April Fool's Day, this was absolutely no joke.

Chapter 23

Our Engagement
(2006–2007)

The time that passed between the day I first met Deb and the day I finally accepted her multiple proposals was just a little over a month. And what a month of absolute joy and unconditional love it had been.

After returning back home after our wonderful weekend in Monterey, the next item on the engagement agenda was the ring. Since I'd never been on the receiving end of an engagement ring before, I wasn't quite sure what Deb had in mind. What I did know was that she was insistent I have a nice ring. She kept saying, "I have a beautiful woman that I am about to marry, and she is going to have an equally beautiful ring." So we made an appointment with a local jeweler whom Deb had known for many years.

As we walked to the jewelry store, Deb said to me, "When we get into the store, I want you to pick out any engagement ring you want. I'm going to see just how much of a 'girly-girl' you really are." I was astounded by her generosity and happily accepted her challenge.

I found a beautiful ring with a nice setting, but I didn't really like the center diamond. Then I saw a nice marquis-cut center stone I liked in another ring, but didn't really care for the setting. So the jeweler offered to take the center stone out of one ring and have it mounted into the setting of the ring I liked. It would be absolutely perfect, but it would take a couple weeks to exchange the stones. I looked at Deb and asked, "Are you sure you want to do this?" She answered me with her big, beautiful smile.

After what seemed like an eternity, the jeweler called to tell us the ring had arrived. When we went to pick it up that very same evening, the jeweler commented, "This might just be the prettiest ring I've ever seen, and it's the style you'd see on a Hollywood movie star." I had to admit it was even more beautiful than I'd expected.

"This ring is bold, bright, and beautiful," Deb said. "Just like my future wife." I blushed at the compliment, and the ring fit perfectly.

With this beautiful ring I was now engaged for the entire world to see.

After our engagement, we took a few months to enjoy each other's company and get to know each other better. We went on lots of dates, and since we both like to travel, we took several weekend mini-vacations around California. We also spent a long holiday weekend in Hawaii, went to Las Vegas and Lake Tahoe, and took a trip to New York City for a few days to see some Broadway shows. I also traveled with Deb on some of her business trips to Virginia, Denver, and San Diego. We got lots of quality time together during these travels.

It was also time for the two of us to meet each other's families. We flew back to the Midwest so Deb could meet my mom, dad, and sister over Mother's Day weekend. Since my parents live in a small town in rural Kansas, the nearest large airport is in Omaha, which just happens to be where my sister, Claudia, lives. After we landed, she picked us up at the airport and we grabbed a quick bite to eat, and then we spent the night at her house.

After breakfast the next morning, we began the three-and-a-half-hour drive to my parents' house in Kansas. After an hour or so of the typical getting-acquainted small talk, as we were driving through the cornfields somewhere in central Nebraska, out of the blue my sister casually asked Deb, "So, what's it like being gay?"

Deb and I were both taken aback, and we glanced at each other with equally surprised faces, as if to say, "Did she really ask that?" But in typical fashion, Deb didn't miss a beat. She replied, "Well, 99 percent of my life is exactly like yours. I go to work, bring home a paycheck, shop for groceries, take care of our house, and pay my taxes. The only thing different in my life is that tiny little 1 percent that goes on behind the closed bedroom door."

To which I quickly added, "And that 1 percent is private, just like it is for you and Terry."

My sister seemed to accept that answer without hesitation, and we completed the remainder of the drive without any additional maladroit moments.

We had a wonderful Mother's Day weekend, which included honoring my mother by going with the whole family to the small church my parents have attended for many years. The church is a typical Midwest fundamentalist Christian church and seems to always require that some "fire and brimstone" be nestled somewhere within the sermon. I sat next to my mother, with Deb on my other side. We both hoped, since this was Mother's Day, that there would be at least some mention of the amazing, unconditional love that a mother feels for her children. Unfortunately, there was not one mention of the word love.

The minister was about halfway through the sermon when he launched into a completely unrelated anti-gay tirade that seemed to come out of nowhere. Although I wasn't surprised, I felt the muscles in my jaw begin to tense, and as the minutes went by I was getting angrier and angrier at the hate and judgment being spat from the pulpit. I am certain my mother felt my discomfort, because she reached over, took my hand, and gently squeezed it as if to say, *It's alright dear, he doesn't know any better.* I was immediately calmed by her gentle and accepting touch.

I don't think this had anything to do with me and Deb being present, as the minister had never met either of us and he was relatively new to the community. It had been fifteen years since my transition, and the local people had long since moved past my transition as being any sort of gossip or news; I don't believe he would have had any way of knowing my history.

I could sense that Deb was getting upset too, but since this was Mother's Day and we had come all the way from California to support my mother on her special day, it was neither the time nor the place to make any sort of scene by confronting the minister or leaving the church mid-sermon. So we both suffered through it.

After the sermon, during the after-church social time, my mother introduced me and Deb to her church friends and to the minister. Here again, almost everyone in the congregation, except the minister, knew my history. And since my mother came to terms with my transition many, many years ago, she now simply introduces me as her daughter.

The minister was quite pleasant, and, I believe, completely oblivious to the fact that I was transgender and that Deb and I were engaged to be married. So, instead of confronting his ignorance and homophobia, we simply smiled, took my mother by the hand, and went on with our Sunday.

Of course, throughout the entire get-acquainted weekend, everyone absolutely loved Deb.

Over the course of the next few months, we had visits from Deb's parents, one of her brothers and his family, and both of my daughters. By the end of it all, it seemed that everyone in the two families was officially on board with our plans to get married.

* * *

It was now time to start organizing the multitude of details that go along with planning a wedding. Since Deb had never been married before, and since my role in this wedding was going to be dramatically different than the role I'd played in my first marriage, we both wanted the event to be the perfect Northern California lesbian wedding.

First came the choice of venue. Neither Deb nor I are religious, so we knew we didn't want to be married in a church. As we contemplated the other types of venues available, we both agreed that we'd like an outdoor wedding. This was California, after all.

I'd always been fascinated by the giant California coastal redwoods, which are ancient forests that have trees almost four hundred feet tall and can be over two thousand years old. But since I'd never actually seen them in person, we took a drive into the nearby mountains between San Jose and the Pacific Coast and visited Big Basin Redwoods State Park so I could experience them firsthand.

Amazing as the trees were, we didn't find the perfect grove of trees that said to us, "Get married here." We knew we'd need to widen our search area.

Muir Woods National Monument is another beautiful forest of redwoods just north of San Francisco. So I took a drive up there one afternoon after a business appointment in the city. Once again, it was beautiful but just didn't "click" as a place for our wedding. I didn't know exactly what I expected to see and feel when finding our perfect wedding spot, but I was confident that I'd know it when I saw it.

So we began to expand our search area even further.

As I did more research on Northern California areas of ancient growth coastal redwoods, I discovered Humboldt Redwoods State Park, about five hours north of San Francisco.

Running along the east edge of the park is the Avenue of the Giants, a thirty-one-mile stretch of road with multiple groves of redwood trees dispersed on either side. It sounded like we'd have lots of areas to choose from, so we knew we'd need to explore it in person. But since it is a significant drive north from the Bay Area, we also knew we'd need to plan a long weekend to allow ample time for exploration.

Labor Day weekend was coming up, so we decided to make a road trip along the Pacific coast then; we could explore the beautiful coastline as well as check out the redwoods. We needed to find a specific location for the wedding, as well as a hotel with a restaurant where we could hold the rehearsal dinner and other wedding-related activities. We weren't yet in a rush, but we did feel that time was of the essence, and we were becoming a bit anxious about finding the right location.

★ ★ ★

When Labor Day weekend finally arrived, we took our time driving up the coast along California State Route 1, also known as the Pacific Coast Highway. It is a breathtaking drive, but certainly not the route to take if you're in a hurry. So we took our time and absorbed as much of the beauty as possible as we meandered northward. We spent the first night on the coast in the quaint little town of Mendocino.

After breakfast the next morning, we continued our trek toward the redwoods and along the way passed many kitschy little tourist attractions. We had a difficult time not stopping at every single one of them, as Deb and I both enjoy these unusual little places. We decided we'd have to make a separate trip at a later date just so we could see them all. Still, try as we might, we simply couldn't resist the Chandelier Drive-Thru tree near Leggett. And of course we took several pictures of Deb's car inside the tree. We are such geeky tourists!

As we entered The Avenue of the Giants, the serenity was immediate, and very much like I had pictured it in my mind. The road that meandered through the giant redwood trees was winding and narrow. Many of the trees actually had reflectors on them, as they sometimes literally defined the edge of the road. The relative darkness of the forest was also striking, as some areas are so dense that the sun never reaches the ground.

I hadn't known until that day of exploration that there were many groves of trees that were named for a particular tree, service club, individual person, or organization that helped save these majestic trees. These remaining groves were saved from the widespread logging that occurred throughout the late nineteenth century and beginning of the twentieth century. Without private and governmental intervention, these ancient trees would have been completely and totally destroyed.

We quickly determined that we would not be able to adequately explore this large and magnificent park in one weekend. Some of the groves were quite expansive and had multiple hiking trails that led from one to another. Some had picnic areas with parking lots, while others did not. But all of the groves had one thing in common: they were breathtakingly beautiful! Now we just had to find the perfect grove for our wedding.

We resigned ourselves to simply enjoying the weekend and exploring the groves and surrounding areas as much as possible while accepting that we would have to come back at a later date to explore even more. One cannot hurry when in such a serene environment. This would be the first of many visits to this wonderful place.

* * *

Now that we knew the general area where we were going to be married, the time had come to start making specific plans. When and how would we decide on a specific date? How many people were we going to invite? Where could we rent a tent for the reception and dance? Where could we rent a generator (since the forest groves don't have any power)? Who was going to cater it? Who would be the photographer? Where would we get the flowers?

Fortunately, Deb's a great organizer and loves making spreadsheets for just about anything she can. So the wedding spreadsheet began.

Then came the decisions about a wedding gown. Should I buy one off the rack or have one custom-made just for me? And if I decided on custom, how would I find a dressmaker? What was our budget? What style did I want? So many decisions!

Not only were there many decisions to be made, I was seeing this wedding from a completely different perspective than my first. Being a bride is a completely different experience from being a groom, of course—but it was much more than that. I didn't get to grow up as a little girl playing with dolls and dressing up like a princess. I didn't get to have slumber parties and play with makeup with my girlfriends. I completely missed out on that part of being a girl. So I had to differentiate between what was unexpressed childhood fantasy and what the expectation for a middle-aged woman getting married for the first time was. But at the same time, if a woman can't express her inner princess at her own wedding, when the heck can she?

After a brief period of inner turmoil, the princess ultimately won. (Much to my delight, I might add.)

It was time to start with the check-off list from Deb's spreadsheet.

It immediately became apparent that it was time to schedule another trip to the redwoods. Item number one was to find the exact location for the wedding so we could start planning details and logistics.

Item number two: Find a nearby hotel and restaurant for the rehearsal dinner and a convenient place for everyone to stay.

So, back to the redwoods we went. Since we'd been there before and now had more knowledge of the overall layout of the many beautiful groves, we were more efficient this time. Of course the grove had to be beautiful and inviting, and far enough from the main road to be serene and peaceful. It also needed to have parking available for the guests, as well as adequate room for the reception tent, florist, caterer, photographer, DJ, and so on. With this list of requirements we could move through the selection process fairly quickly.

Many of the groves were simply too small, and others were too close to the main road. And then we found the gem we were looking for. It was appropriately named "The California Federation of Women's Clubs Grove." We had driven by it on our previous trip but hadn't actually noticed it because it is marked only by a relatively small sign and is set well back from the main highway. It is at the end of a narrow, winding road that meanders through the redwoods and ends up next to the Eel River. It also has a beautiful four-fireplace Hearthstone monument designed by famous Bay Area architect Julia Morgan. We both immediately knew that we'd found just the right place.

There were clean restrooms, a nice large parking lot, and lots of beautiful redwoods right next to the river. And since it was nearly a half-mile away from the main highway, other than the peaceful nature sounds, it was completely silent. In a word, it was perfect!

Now all we needed to find was a hotel for our guests and a restaurant for the rehearsal dinner.

We remembered driving by a lovely hotel called the Benbow Inn on both our last trip to the redwoods and this most recent one. It seemed to be conveniently located: just a few miles from the entrance to Avenue of the Giants and outside a little town called Garberville. We decided to check it out and see if it met our requirements—and wow, did it ever! It was absolutely beautiful. It was built in 1926 and was on the National Register of Historic Places. It was built in the traditional English Tudor style, with a spacious, elegant, dark wood lobby and large fireplace. Adjacent to the lobby, the pub-style bar was equally comfortable and inviting. And, as a full-service hotel, it also offered a restaurant and meeting room for our rehearsal dinner. The guest rooms were outstanding and many of them also had wood-burning fireplaces. It, too, was perfect.

Knowing a beautiful place like this would likely have many weddings scheduled throughout the year, we decided to see what dates might be available. Not surprisingly, all the summer weekends were already taken up with either weddings or other large-scale events. So we inquired about the early fall—and fortunately, the weekend after Labor Day was still available and sounded just right for our ceremony.

Early September in Northern California is just about the perfect wedding weather, with warm daytime temperatures and cool nights. Plus, it almost never rains in September. So we booked the weekend of September 8th, 2007.

We'd done it; we now had our wedding date! But once we got back to Pleasanton, the real work began. Fortunately, we were both up to the task with Deb's wedding planner spreadsheet already in hand. Deb started calling the various vendors we would require, and I started researching my wedding gown.

I asked my good friend from Denver, Rachel, to be my maid of honor, and then asked my two daughters to be bridesmaids. Since our colors were black, white, and red, I asked Rachel to wear a nice black suit (she doesn't like to wear dresses), and then invited my daughters to come up to San Francisco so we could shop for their bridesmaids' dresses. I wanted the dresses to be elegant as well as something they could wear for semi-formal events after the wedding. I also wanted their help in choosing a wedding gown, so we also scheduled the time to visit a few bridal shops while we were in the city. Fortunately there is a large upscale mall in the Union Square area of San Francisco, and several bridal shops are located on nearby Maiden Lane. How convenient!

We shopped at the mall for the bridesmaids' dresses for a couple of hours and then went to a few of the nearby bridal shops to look at wedding gowns. I tried on several beautiful gowns, but nothing really spoke to me. If I was going to spend the amount of money that would be required for just the right dress, it needed to be absolutely perfect.

So we went back to the mall, had lunch, and discussed our options. After lunch we went back to reevaluate one of the first dresses the girls had tried on—a simple black, strapless, below-the-knee, satin evening dress—and decided that it would be just right. It was both elegant and versatile. Then we chose some dark red, patent leather, open-toed, low-platform high heels to compliment the dresses.

We then drove to a custom dress and corset shop called Dark Garden Corsetry and Couture. We were quite impressed with the quality of their corsets, and spent some time looking through several books of custom wedding gowns they had made for other brides. The owner, Autumn, was very friendly and answered many of our questions. Happy with the experience, I scheduled an appointment for an in-depth consultation the following week. After a day of shopping, it had become apparent that I wasn't going to be happy with an off-the-rack wedding gown.

After my daughters returned home to Southern California, I spent several days looking at wedding gowns online, trying to pick out various styles that appealed to me. I didn't really know what to expect from my upcoming gown design consultation at Dark Garden, so I wanted to have some general ideas to present to Autumn. I printed off several pictures, and eventually came to the conclusion that I definitely wanted a corset top with a crinoline-supported, princess-like flared bottom.

Other than an inexpensive Halloween costume bodice, I had never owned a real corset. I had no idea why I was drawn to that particular article of clothing; I only knew that I was. So, since this was to be the fairy-tale wedding of my dreams, I was determined to explore every possible avenue to make my dream day come true. I assume that since all the princesses in all the fairy-tale books are slender-waisted and have elaborate satin gowns with large flared bottoms, at a subconscious level, this was simply part of my fairy-tale fantasy. And what better place to explore this fantasy interest than an actual corset shop in San Francisco?

I wanted an elegant and somewhat traditional look, with a bit of nineteenth-century feeling thrown in for good measure. I still had no idea how my concepts would turn into a beautiful wedding gown, however.

When I met with Autumn at Dark Garden, she amazed me with her skill. She looked at the pictures I'd brought with me, asked some questions about other specific ideas I had, and then started sketching on an artist's pad for clarification. She would draw what she thought I was describing and then make changes as the concepts became clearer to both of us. I knew I wanted a lot of lace, using the primary color of satin white with some black accents. I also knew I wanted a little bit of red added for flair but didn't yet know how that could be judiciously added. Autumn's ability to sketch overall concepts with minute detail as we spoke amazes me to this day. In just a matter of minutes she had sketched out an overall pattern for a gown that would make my princess wedding day come true. My feet hardly touched the ground as I left her store; I was filled with anticipation and delight.

In the following months and throughout the multiple fitting appointments, the attention to detail and overall elegance of the process became apparent as Autumn and her talented staff of corsetières and dressmakers turned her simple sketch

into the wedding gown of my dreams. We ultimately decided to use red satin for the back center panel in the middle of my long, flowing train. That way, as I walked down the aisle, our guests would initially see a very beautiful traditional white lace gown from the front, and as I passed by and moved to ceremonial center stage, they'd see the beautiful red accent in back. It was absolutely stunning!

While I was happily occupied with all the excitement of having my dress made, Deb was busy with her spreadsheet, taking care of the other, less glamorous items that would be necessary to create a wedding and reception in the middle of an ancient forest. Her tasks revolved around things such as locating and renting quiet yet powerful electrical generators, calculating extension cord power loss, determining the combined wattage of evening party lights, coffee makers, DJ amplifiers, and food warmers, and more.

During this time, one of the potential photographers Deb contacted told her, "We do not *do* same-sex weddings!"

Deb was unfazed and simply moved on to another photographer. We were both angry about this blatant display of discrimination, but we weren't about to allow the bigotry of one narrow-minded homophobe to ruin our entire wedding planning process, so we quickly moved past it—and Deb soon found a photographer who was not only willing to photograph a same-sex wedding, he was quite excited about it. He said he would bring two additional photographers along to make certain they got every conceivable shot, and then he asked permission to use our wedding photos in his future marketing. We were honored and consented to his request.

With a few more phone calls, Deb found an equally cooperative caterer and florist, as well as a local rental company that would deliver and construct the reception tent in the parking lot adjacent to our ceremony.

Since the grove was within the boundaries of a California State Park, we also had to research what was required to reserve a space for a private event. The online website was quite helpful, and the administrators who answered the phones were also friendly. State Park policies, they told us, stated that the spots were reserved first come, first served, and the reservation required a relatively minimal administrative fee. Fortunately, the weekend after Labor Day of the following year was still open. We immediately reserved it. We had our venue!

Not only were the park rangers always very professional during our interactions, they seemed quite excited to host a same-sex wedding ceremony within the boundaries of their park. After all, this was the California Federation of Women's Clubs Grove, and it seemed like the perfect setting for a lesbian wedding.

It's a good thing we started making all these arrangements nearly a year in advance, because even with Deb's superb spreadsheet organizational skills, we found that planning a wedding at a remote location took a *lot* of time and energy.

As the wedding date drew nearer, there was still the issue of my hair. I had a wonderful hairdresser named Jane, who worked out of her home in the Bay Area, but we were going to be in Humboldt County a couple of days in advance of the actual wedding date, five hours away. And I certainly wasn't going to trust a new local hairdresser at a nearby salon for this important event. It was time to resurrect one of my human hair wigs.

I hadn't been wearing a wig, or any sort of hair replacement system, for several years at this point. But this seemed like the perfect time to resort to that level of pre-planning. So I made arrangements with Jane to style and hairspray my wig several days before our wedding so I could simply take my "hair in a box" and put it on my head for the wedding. It worked wonderfully!

Deb's spreadsheet checklist was now complete. It was time to load up the station wagon and assemble all the puzzle pieces on-site at the Benbow Inn and at the Women's Grove in the park.

Our wedding day was almost here!

Chapter 24

The Wedding
(2007)

We arrived at the Benbow Inn on Thursday afternoon, two days before the wedding, which would take place on Saturday. The rehearsal and dinner were scheduled for Friday afternoon and evening, so we had lots of things to organize before that time.

All of the vendors we'd hired were wonderful, and everything fell into place without incident. The park rangers were kind enough to sweep the parking lot of the grove so the tent rental people had a nice clean place to erect the tent. And while they couldn't stop people from entering the state park during our ceremony, the ranger we spoke to said the presence of our tent, multiple parked cars, and people walking around dressed in formal clothes would most likely dissuade anyone from interfering. They also said they'd be sure to add a couple extra patrols throughout the day to be sure nobody bothered anything.

Everyone arrived in plenty of time for the Friday afternoon rehearsal, and both the rehearsal and evening dinner were relaxed, informal, and a wonderful time for friends and family to intermingle. Both sets of parents came for our special celebration, mine from Kansas and Deb's from Southern California. This was the first time they'd met.

On the morning of the wedding, Deb and I had an early breakfast together, but parted ways after that; we had decided to be quite traditional and not let her see me as I got ready for the ceremony, safely cloistered in the room of Rachel, my maid of honor. My oldest daughter, Nikki, had agreed to do my makeup and any necessary touchups on my hair, while Autumn, the talented dressmaker and owner of Dark Garden, had graciously agreed to be my dresser. That part of the day couldn't have been more elegant or luxurious. We sipped champagne, posed a few times throughout the process for the photographer, and had a delightful time.

After completing my three-hour fairy princess transformation with hair, makeup, and my absolutely amazing wedding gown, the photographers took us around the Benbow Inn garden-like grounds for some pre-ceremony photos. They had already photographed Deb and her family in many of the same locations, and assured us she was no longer on the Benbow grounds. After all, we certainly couldn't let her see me now!

I was then escorted to the awaiting limousine, and my entourage and I were whisked away from the Benbow Inn and off to the redwood grove. I could already tell the time was rushing by way too quickly. I wanted to shout, "Slow down! I need more time to enjoy this!"

When we turned off the main highway and onto the winding road leading to the Women's Grove, the moments became even more magical. As we drove by the big white reception tent and over to the long red carpet leading into the forest and all the way to the ceremonial site, my personal fairy tale continued to unfold. It was so beautiful I could hardly believe my eyes.

As I climbed out of the limo, I needed considerable help from Nikki, Erika, and Rachel in managing and unfolding my large bell-shaped wedding dress with its stiff crinoline frame, long train, and flowing veil. It took all three of them to keep the fabric off the ground and help carry the many yards of material across the edge of the forest floor and over to the carpet, where it could then be smoothed and arranged.

It was time to take a long, deep breath and try to relax as I waited for the music to announce my entry.

★ ★ ★

As Georgia the DJ began to play "Here Comes the Bride," I started my step-by-step walk down the one hundred-and-fifty-foot red carpet that Deb had specially purchased and carefully laid across the forest floor just for our wedding. Everyone was now standing, and they all turned to watch me come down the aisle. As the carpet made a gradual turn from the parking lot and then on to the ceremonial grove, I was able to see Deb standing at the very end with a smile that was bigger than any smile I had ever seen before. She was absolutely radiant!

She was surrounded by our entire wedding party, which consisted of my bridesmaid, Rachel; my daughters, Nikki and Erika; Deb's "best woman" and sister, Denise; and our good friend and minister, Kelli. The chairs on either side of the aisle held a relatively small but wonderful group—approximately fifty-five of our closest friends from across the country, both sets of parents, and other family members—in this intimate and sacred, millenniums-old grove of ancient trees. It was a breathtaking sight to behold.

As I reached the ceremonial area in front and took Debbie's hand in mine, Kelli began the wedding ceremony. The ceremony was traditional and included two songs sung by Nikki, along with an exchange of rings and reading of the vows that Deb and I had written to each other.

We'd known that in the nervous moments of the ceremony we might forget our vows, so we'd had them typewritten on separate pieces of paper so we could actually read them if that became necessary. And we were indeed nervous enough to not trust our memories, so Deb read her vows first and then I reached into the corset top of my gown to retrieve mine. All seemed innocent enough until I realized I couldn't read the words on my paper because I wasn't wearing my eyeglasses. I burst into laughter, as everyone in the audience could see exactly what was happening. Fortunately, I was able to hold the paper at arms' length, and between the few words I could actually read and the little bit of memory I still had, I somehow managed to recite my vows.

After the ceremony, we moved from the chapel-like area to our nearby reception tent, where the party was about to really begin. The caterers brought out an amazing assortment of different foods, salads, and delicious appetizers, along with a wonderful variety of California wines and artisanal beers. It was apparent that nobody was going to leave this wedding hungry.

After Deb and I had our first dance together as a married couple, DJ Georgia began to spin a delightful assortment of music that seemed to please just about everyone. The dance floor filled quickly, and everyone was having a fabulous time.

There were many toasts that brought tears to our eyes as our family and friends shared their loving thoughts—speeches that will stay with us forever. We also had a traditional wedding cake ceremony, and Deb and I both promised not to embarrass each other with the cutting of the cake and feeding each other the first bite. Fortunately, we both kept our promises.

The eating, drinking, dancing, and merriment continued for several hours, and the wedding day simply could not have gone better.

As the caterers began to wind down at the end of the event, one of the managers came over to speak with Deb. She told her that they cater weddings all the time and have done hundreds of weddings throughout the years. She said that of all the weddings they'd ever done, our wedding was the most unconditionally loving. What a wonderful compliment!

We had friends and family in attendance from places as far away as Chicago, Omaha, Denver, and Kansas. Since our wedding was a celebration of love with our extended family, our families and attending guests had demonstrated their unconditional love and acceptance simply by being in joyous celebration with those identifying as straight, lesbian, gay, bisexual, cisgender, transgender, Christian, Jew, Pagan, Wiccan, Democrat, Republican, Green, multiracial, multicultural, and everything in between. And with such an amazingly diverse group of people represented, there was nothing but a complete demonstration of amazing love, respect, and acceptance for all. Peace was the order of the day.

★ ★ ★

Of course, no wedding is complete without an after-party. The wedding and reception in the forest began to wind down as the sun set behind the nearby coastal mountains, so the party moved to the pub at the Benbow Inn.

After Deb and I came back from the redwoods, we headed to our room so I could take off my wedding gown. But first, Deb wanted to stop by the pub and make sure everything was ready. I was standing outside the pub in the adjacent courtyard when a thirty-something mother with two young daughters happened by. The younger daughter was about five or so, and as she saw me standing there in my elaborate gown her eyes grew to the size of silver dollars, and she eagerly asked, "Are you a *real* princess?" I looked at her and answered, "Yes I am," as I lifted my arms and spun a complete circle in front of her. Her mouth dropped wide open as her mother smiled at me and moved her and her sister down the hall.

After going back to our room, Deb exchanged her suit for some more comfortable clothes and I took off my heels, wig, and wedding skirt. I put on a pair of denim shorts over the top of my white panty hose, put my wedding garter on my right thigh, and donned my pink fuzzy bedroom slippers. We called my casual/elegant look "Princess Down!"

As fate would have it, as we were walking out of our room and up the stairs to the pub, the same mother-daughter trio came around the corner. The littlest girl again looked at me with fascination, pointed at my thigh, and asked, "Is that a *real* garter?" I answered, "Yes it is," and let her touch the frilly bow. I am quite sure our wedding day was a day that little girl will also remember for the rest of her life.

The after-party was a wonderful time to casually socialize and continue to converse with our amazing group of family and friends, all of whom had taken time out of their busy schedules to make the trip to our wedding. So many people had come from out of town, or had committed to the five-hour drive and long weekend to celebrate us, and we didn't take anyone's attendance lightly. The outpouring of love and support continued for the remainder of the evening, and when it was finally time to call it a day, Deb and I returned to our room knowing full well that we had surrounded ourselves with the most amazing group of people imaginable. What a wonderful way to end a fairy-tale day!

Chapter 25

My Next Chapter in Life?
(2007)

I believe life is a series of chapters. My next chapter of my life can quite simply be called NuMoon. NuMoon is the name of our most recent journey forward in life: a forty-two-foot yacht. And while she's new to us, she's actually a 1984 Nova Sundeck. Since she's a "trawler-style" yacht with twin 135hp diesel engines, she doesn't go anywhere quickly, but she can efficiently cruise for a very long time on one tank of fuel.

As I get older, I am becoming more aware that as we go through life (and boating) the journey is every bit as important as the final destination. Getting there quickly is not so important. So from our current perspective, speed is reserved for cars and airplanes, not motor yachts and life.

Even though Debbie and I have been together for nearly two years now, we only recently discovered that we have both long yearned for a boat you could live on. We both wanted a large boat because having the ability to move aboard and sail away gives you a feeling of freedom and opens up a whole new realm of possibilities. And since it was an unexpressed desire for both of us, once we discussed it and became receptive to the possibility, the Universe happily and quickly fulfilled our desire. NuMoon came happily into our life soon afterward, and immediately expanded our horizons.

And as a not-so-coincidental side note, metaphysically speaking, the New Moon represents "planting the seeds of your next dream." So even the name of the boat was perfect.

We originally planned for our honeymoon to be a two-week Mediterranean cruise, but after we bought NuMoon, we decided instead to spend our entire seventeen-day honeymoon cruising our own boat through the inland waterways of the San Francisco Bay and California Delta.

In the meantime, keep dreaming your dreams and know that *anything* is possible if you simply *believe*!

MY CURRENT PERSPECTIVE

Deb and I have now been together for ten years, are still quite active in boating, and still own NuMoon. We are actively involved with the Barbary Coast Boating Club, a Bay Area gay yacht club, and spend many summer weekends and most major holidays cruising to remote Delta locations for fun and boating frolic.

Since NuMoon is such a substantial boat, people often ask if either of us have ever owned a boat before. While the answer is technically no, Deb and I have been peripherally involved in boating since we were children. I had an uncle in Kansas who had a ski boat, and the highlight of my summer was when we would meet with his family at a nearby reservoir and I would get to drive his boat while others water-skied behind us. As an adult I had various friends who owned ski boats or sailboats, so summer boating was still a relatively frequent activity. I even raced Hobie Cats with a friend for a few summers while living in Colorado.

As for Deb, her father had a small fishing boat when she was growing up, so he would trailer that boat to nearby lakes and occasionally go out to the ocean so they could fish and camp. So she grew up being active in boating as well.

In regards to who drives the boat—that responsibility usually rests with me. Since I grew up on a farm where I operated tractors, trucks, combines, and more, and since I'm also a licensed private pilot, for me, a large boat is simply just another piece of heavy equipment. And remarkably enough, there are many similarities between flying and boating.

Recently, we recently bought our retirement home in a 55+ community in Rio Vista, which is also in the Delta, only ten miles from where we keep NuMoon. So I guess you could say we're officially Delta girls now.

After growing up in a small, rural Kansas town, Rio Vista feels very much like home to me. Recently my youngest daughter, Erika, came to visit us in our new home. As we were driving through the farmlands from the Sacramento airport to our house, she commented, "Wow, you have really gone back to your roots!" Even she recognized the similarities between California farmlands and Kansas farmlands. And I don't think that's necessarily a bad thing.

Chapter 26

My Evolution to Second Mom Status
(2007)

When I first began my transition from male to female back in 1999, one of the things I promised my daughters was that I would always be their "Daddy"—and that regardless of my physical presentation, state of transition, or living arrangements with their mother or another woman, I would always be available for them.

At the beginning of my transition, they called me "Daddy" or "Dad" and often struggled with the feminine pronoun when used in the same sentence. As time passed, with persistent and consistent practice, the correct pronoun came easier and easier.

Within months, when introducing me to their friends, they would not hesitate to say something like, "This is Alexus, she's my dad."

As you can probably imagine, this made for some interesting conversations, as unknowing friends would often later ask something like, "Now, who is Alexus, and how do you know her?"

When we were out in public, most people would logically assume I was my daughters' mother. This could create a bit of a challenge. Even though it felt out of integrity to simply go along with the misassumption, it was much easier to let it slide, so I often did. Sometimes the girls would correct people by saying, "She's my aunt." Either way, we were stuck between dishonoring their biological mother and lying by omission, or dishonoring my parental relationship with them by calling me their aunt. It hurt every time it happened.

For three years of our five-year relationship, Cristina and I raised her daughter, Emily, together. At the time Emily moved in with us, she was four years old and always referred to me as "Mommy Number Two." My relationship with Emily was, and still is, quite close. She and I had a particularly tight connection because she sometimes felt she could confide in me in ways she could not to her birth mom.

When Emily was in kindergarten, because Cristina was working full-time, I was the stay-at-home mom and met Emily at the bus every afternoon. I would walk her home, talk with her about school, and fix her a snack before she met up with friends or watched cartoons. This gave us additional quality time together and helped me adjust to my role as a maternal parent much quicker. And since I never acted as a father figure to her, I didn't have as many behavior patterns to unlearn. I really did feel like I was a second mother to her and I liked that feeling. After my relationship with Cristina ended, I grieved not only the loss of the relationship with her but the loss of Emily as well.

After the breakup, and in the year prior to moving to California, I lived alone. This was a particularly valuable, albeit difficult, time for me; I learned a great deal about myself. I think one of the reasons it was so valuable for my personal growth was that I chose not to date or pursue any sort of romantic relationship. And while I kept somewhat busy with my courier job, I was often alone—alone to ponder the meaning of my new life; alone to ponder my new societal and familial roles; alone to discover the next great chapter in my life.

One of the discoveries I made during this time was how much I enjoyed being with my daughters. I went on a two-week cruise with Erika, and then a few months later helped her find an apartment when she moved to Hollywood. After that, I went to New York and spent two weeks with Nikki. Soon thereafter, Erika returned to Colorado for a surgery and she stayed with me during her recovery.

As time went by, and as I settled into simply "being" a middle-aged single woman, I gradually evolved into a more confident, loving, and gentle person. And as my personal changes occurred, my relationship with my daughters changed and grew.

In the fall of 2005, I moved to the San Francisco Bay Area to start my job in corporate sales. A bonus was that I would get to be closer to Erika, who was still in Hollywood.

Then, in July of 2006, after going on a one-year national tour with the Broadway show *Joseph and the Amazing Technicolor Dreamcoat*, Nikki also moved to Hollywood and moved in with Erika. That meant I had *both* my daughters living just a one-hour flight away. Hooray!

Over the years since my transition, a great deal has changed in my life. Since the changes have occurred gradually, and have typically been assimilated unnoticed, it has sometimes taken a significant moment for my awareness of the change to crystallize.

This happened for me about a month ago when I was again visiting my daughters in LA. We were out shopping when one of the clerks casually asked Erika about our relationship, assuming I was her mother. Erika responded with the usual, "No, she's my aunt"—and in this moment, I became acutely aware of the need for a different response. As we walked away I asked the girls if we could consider a different response. I asked them if the words "second mom" or the name "Mom Number Two" would feel appropriate to them. They both immediately agreed that they would.

I am aware that I am not my daughters' biological mother. They already have one of those, and she's a wonderful person and loving mother. I know I did not endure pregnancy, give birth, or nurse my children when they were babies. Neither was I their primary parent when they were growing up.

But motherhood is not simply about giving birth. There are many wonderful mothers who have never given birth to a child. And there are many "mothers" who have performed the biological function of giving birth but do not adequately fulfill the remaining requisite functions of motherhood. Being a true mother is about being a consistently loving, supportive, emotionally available parent and role model for your children. I believe I now fit that description quite well, and apparently my children agree.

We have since had the opportunity to use the "Second

Mom" description during various introductions, and it has always been accepted without hesitation. After all, there are many blended families nowadays, given how commonplace divorce, stepparents, adoptions, same-sex parents, and a whole variety of other family descriptions are.

What I now know for certain is that I love both my daughters deeply and I am very proud of them. Not only have they effectively coped with some extremely difficult circumstances in life, they have grown and thrived. And through it all, they have been two of the most amazing and unconditionally loving women I know.

For us, "Mom Number Two" works. Not only does it feel more authentic and allow us to stay in complete integrity, it feels like a natural evolution.

MY CURRENT PERSPECTIVE

This is still a work in process. The "second mom" title seems to work when we're out in public and interacting with strangers, but when we're together in private my daughters simply call me Alexus, which feels a little distant for my liking. I have told them I don't mind if they call me "Dad" when we're in a private setting, but since they've been calling me Alexus for nearly fifteen years now, they're fine with it as it is. (At least for now.)

Chapter 27

When Did I Know?

20/20 Episode Sparks 20/20 Hindsight
(2007)

After the 2007 ABC airing of a new *20/20* with Barbara Walters—an episode in which Barbara interviews the families of several transgender children—I sent the YouTube link to my mom and sister. After watching the entire program, my mother called me up and asked, "When did you know you wanted to be a girl?"

I had to give this some thought, and in response to her question, I penned the following letter and sent it to my parents and sister, Claudia. As strange as it may seem, especially since I've had some version of a website for over a decade, I had never before written about my earliest memories regarding all things gender related.

With my mother's loving consent, here is the letter I wrote:

Hi Mom and Dad,

I'm glad you finally got to watch the entire show. Yes, Barbara did do a great job on it. And I'm quite sure you can relate to all the parents' feelings. I thought of you both when I watched it. And thank you for asking about my early transgender feelings. We've really never discussed this before and I always wanted to share my feelings with you . . .

I knew at a very early age that something was significantly "wrong" or "different" about me. I just never seemed to fit in with the rest of the kids. No matter what I did with them, or which group I was with, I always felt like an outsider.

As soon as I could read and comprehend the encyclopedias at White Eagle (and there were two complete sets), I began to read everything I could find on transsexuality, transvestism, and hermaphrodism (now called intersex). And even though I did not yet comprehend that I was reading about myself, I would always hide behind the outhouse or shield the pages from others while reading those sections. And when you would drop me at the city library on Saturdays while you were shopping I would read those encyclopedias too. There, I always hid in the darkest and most remote corner so nobody could see what I was reading. So since there was some subconscious shame about the topic, I obviously identified with "something" transgender at an early age. The other interesting thing was that by the time I went into town school in fifth grade, I already knew all about Christine Jorgensen and also knew if you wanted a sex-change operation in the US you'd go to

Trinidad, Colorado. These are not things that most eight- to twelve-year-old farm boys would typically care about.

And even though I could never articulate my inner feelings, I always admired Claudia and worshipped the ground she walked on. I always wanted to be just like her. And when she went through puberty and began to develop into a woman, I was very, very jealous. When I was alone in the bathroom as a child I would often "tuck" my genitals back between my legs so I could see what I would look like as a girl. I did that a LOT and I liked what I saw! And when Claudia would have other girls over to spend the night and/or go to all-girl parties, I was always SO envious of her. I thought girl-talk was just the best thing going and I would eavesdrop whenever I could. (I'm sure she remembers that.)

But again, these are not things a Kansas farm boy tells his parents . . . or anyone else for that matter.

In regards to childhood cross-dressing, I didn't do that very much because it felt too dangerous, but when you and Dad were both out of the house, and I knew you'd be gone for a while, I would sometimes sneak into your closet and wear your high heel shoes and frilly nightgowns.

I'm sure you also remember how much I liked to sew as a child and I don't think it is coincidental that my first significant sewing project was a pink shirt. And later my racecar was, of course, PINK! You probably also remember the time as a teenager that I dressed up like a girl for Halloween. What you don't know is that I enjoyed that immensely and it somehow felt WAY too natural.

As a teenager and into adulthood, I still struggled to find my place in life. It seemed that I got lots of accolades by being an overachiever in everything I did, so that seemed to be the best route for me and helped me distract from that "inner feeling" of angst. But whenever there was *a party or gathering of friends, I would always end up in the kitchen with the women, enjoying that conversation over whatever the men were talking about elsewhere. And even when I was with the guys, some of my male friends would occasionally comment about the way I sat when I was relaxed. One of them even once said, "You sit like a GIRL!" Of course I did not then know why that was so natural for me. And strangely enough, now my lesbian friends tease me about the same thing. They say things like, "You're such a girl. I could never sit like that."*

The rest of my adult story you've probably already read from my website so there's nothing really new there.

Thank you for recognizing that I'm now very happy with who I am. I am more at peace with myself than I've ever been in my entire life and I absolutely LOVE the woman I've become. (But then again, I had two amazing and wonderful female role models throughout my entire childhood.)

Thank you again for loving and supporting me as I really was meant to be. Not all parents are as strong and as loving as you. This is what my life was supposed to feel like! And I'm happy to be here.

Much Love,
Alexus

MY CURRENT PERSPECTIVE

This seemed to be a very clarifying letter (and TV show) for both my parents. I think it gave them more insight into some of the deep-seated feelings with which I had struggled for most of my life. Since most transgender people are very good at hiding their conflicted feelings regarding gender identity, along with any trans-related cross-dressing activities, it is no wonder that most people are quite surprised when we finally "come out" to them.

They say that "time heals all wounds." I didn't write this letter to my parents until nearly ten years after I first came out to them. While they did struggle in the early years of my transition, by the time this letter was written, they had pretty much come to terms with having another daughter.

Chapter 28

Living and Cruising Aboard Our Yacht
(2008)

In March 2008, the company Deb had been working for was purchased. Since she held a senior-level position, she was offered a "buy-out" to retire early. And while she's not yet ready to retire permanently, she did want to take the opportunity to take at least a yearlong sabbatical. So that's what we're doing! We're living and cruising aboard our forty-two-foot motor yacht, NuMoon.

Last May we left our homeport of Alameda, CA and cruised up the coast to the Pacific Northwest. We spent a month in the San Juan Islands of Washington and then another month in Canada cruising the Gulf Islands, Princess Louisa Inlet, and Desolation Sound. We then turned back south for another month in Puget Sound before cruising back down the coast to Alameda.

After spending nearly two months in Northern California, we started our winter journey; first down to Southern California, and then on to Mexico after the first of the year.

I know this section has nothing to do with being transgender, but fortunately, not everything in life is about gender. I also hope our journey will help you be inspired to reach for *your* dreams! That's the only way they'll come to you . . .

Namaste.

MY CURRENT PERSPECTIVE
Deb and I lived aboard NuMoon for four years and actively cruised the Pacific West Coast and Sea of Cortez for two of those years. This meant being together in a very small, confined space twenty-four hours a day, seven days a week, three hundred and sixty-five days a year.

When we moved onto the boat, we were moving out of a three-bedroom, two-bath, ranch-style home of just under two thousand square feet and into a multilevel, trawler-style boat of about four hundred square feet. And while the boat did have three state rooms (bedrooms) and two heads (bathrooms), most of the rooms weren't much bigger than our house's walk-in closet had been. Downsizing for such a move was an event in and of itself.

Even with the significant adjustments that living in such a confined and constantly moving space required, the sense of freedom and adventure we enjoyed was something most people can only dream of. Our friends frequently reminded us that we were "living the dream" and should savor every moment. And savor we did . . .

But along with what many saw as a glamorous lifestyle came the day-to-day realities of being constantly on the move and maintaining this incredibly complex vessel. When you live in a house, you are connected to city systems that ensure you have safe and drinkable water coming in and sewage going out. You're always connected to a reliable source of electricity and Internet. On a boat, in contrast, everything is self-contained and every single system requires ongoing maintenance. The "glamour" fades fairly quickly when dealing with these systems, which at times can be frustrating and cause tempers to flare.

What Debbie and I learned while being together in such a small space for a very long time is that we're quite compatible and have a great deal of love and respect for each other. That's not to say that we didn't have our share of arguments and occasionally needed to spend some time on opposite ends of the boat, but ultimately we knew there was no escape from the issues and we had to come to terms with whatever was bothering us. As a result, it deepened our relationship. We were more deeply in love with one another after that journey than when we began it.

We also learned that the marine community in general is simply not used to seeing two women handling a relatively large vessel by themselves.

Like an airplane landing, no two dockings are ever the same—so we always had an organized plan in mind going into a docking, while at the same time preparing ourselves to immediately change those plans as winds, currents, or other unseen docking issues might dictate in the moment. So it could be an unpredictable and sometimes-stressful few minutes.

When coming into a potentially complex docking situation, as I was positioning the vessel, Deb would be on the foredeck handling the lines and getting ready to tie us to the dock. If there happened to be someone nearby who offered to take the lines, she would tell them where and how she wanted them tied. They would often take the approach that because they were men they must know better how and where we should tie our lines. But since Deb and I had already planned exactly how we were going to dock, and those plans usually relied on a specific line being tied at a specific location on the dock, this was neither the time nor place for a discussion with an uninformed but well-meaning stranger on the dock.

At first, Deb would cheerfully but specifically direct them where to tie the line. As long as they complied with her request, there was no issue. But if they resisted or otherwise delayed the task, Deb would quickly change her tone and become insistent. If they still resisted, she would demand that they immediately toss her back the line and she'd tie it from the boat herself. This was a scene that repeated itself many times over the course of our two years of cruising. We found that the men on the dock were simply not used to taking orders from a strong woman like Deb.

On another occasion, we had the opportunity to visit a very pretty and touristy town in Washington with two women friends who were visiting us for a few days. The town was positioned on the edge of a narrow tidal channel between the mainland and a nearby island. The current in the channel could be quite significant, and it switched direction four times a day along with the changing tides.

Since our friends were eager to help, and had already been aboard for a couple days at this point, we pre-planned our docking with the welcome help of their additional hands. As a result, even though the current was substantial at the time we came in, the docking went flawlessly.

As we turned off the engines and secured the boat in preparation for going ashore, we heard someone clapping their hands from somewhere nearby. We looked around to find the source of the applause and saw a man up on the roof of a restaurant adjacent to the dock.

"Nice job, ladies!" he called down. He then informed us that he'd been working on that roof all day and had seen several boats come and go throughout those hours. "That was by far the best docking I've seen all day!" he said. "Now tell me again why we can't have a woman for president?"

We often visited a nearby yacht club after docking our boat at the end of a long day of cruising. Almost every time we sat down at the bar, ordered a drink, and began making small talk, the bartender would ask, "Where are your husbands?" We would tell them there were no husbands, to which they would usually say something to the effect of, "Oh, I see, your husbands are still on the boat?" And we would again say, "No, there *are* no husbands!"

At that point we could usually see the light go on in their mind. "Oh," they would say, recognition dawning, "*now* I understand what you mean by 'there are no husbands.'"

We would simply smile and nod in agreement, and move on to another topic.

The stories of our two years cruising together could easily fill another entire book. But for the purposes of this book, suffice it to say that Deb and I had an absolutely magnificent time together over those two years. It was a sabbatical, the likes of which most people can only dream of. Not only did it deepen our relationship and strengthen our marriage, we truly were "living the dream," just as our friends and family kept telling us. And the experience was truly something we will never forget.

Chapter 29

My TV Debut
(2010)

Life is SO Bizarre!!!
This picture was taken after taping a new show on the Game Show Network called *Baggage*. Jerry Springer was the host, my daughter Nikki was a "dater" contestant, and I was the secret "baggage" she had to reveal at the end of the show.

Never in my life did I expect to utter the words, "I met Jerry Springer today." And I would have found it even less likely to add the statements, "Jerry Springer is a very nice man. I like him very much." But I can truly confirm I said all of that. Go figure!

But I guess I shouldn't be surprised. If there's anything I have learned from my journey through this bizarre life of self-discovery and spiritual adventure, it's that nothing is as it seems!

So here's how it happened:

Today I went with my oldest daughter, Nikki, to the taping of a new game show that will air on the Game Show Network (GSN). The show is called *Baggage*, and it is a dating show where the contestants have to reveal some of the personal "baggage" that has created issues in their dating and relationship lives in the past.

Nikki was the "dater," meaning she was to choose from three potential dates and listen to their baggage (some true, some fictional) before making a choice. And then, after she made her decision, she had to reveal *her* secret baggage. Her secret was, "My father is a woman." Then the guy had the choice to accept the date or decline.

Since I was in the audience watching the show, they invited me onto the stage to "verify" the baggage. Needless to say, the ending went well and the guy didn't freak out at all.

For me, the serendipitous (and strangest) part of it all is that the show host was none other than Jerry Springer. And it turns out that he's a *very* nice man! Who knew?

(Oh yes, and BTW, this is my first appearance on national television!)

MY CURRENT PERSPECTIVE

Even though we've come a long way in the movement to normalize acceptance of the transgender community, at the time this show was taped, it was still quite sensational to have someone openly transgender in your family. The fact that my mere existence was somehow "baggage" that Nikki needed to reveal to a potential date is an indication of just how fringe our situation was still perceived to be. And though we've gradually improved that perception, the fact that we are a very small percentage of the overall population means we will likely remain a curiosity to many people for a long time to come. Hopefully it will someday become just another variation within the spectrum of humanity, akin to something as innocent as having two different-colored eyes.

Chapter 30

The Dilemma of Hair
(2014)

Hair is important to most women, but it is a really big deal for transgender women. It's important because our society assigns gender to everyone (an assignment that's usually subconscious and nearly instantaneous), and hair is one of the distinctions used to differentiate male versus female—so for those of us that are transgender, it is essential to present ourselves such that people who see us will automatically assign the mental gender of female. While makeup can also be very important, hair can be seen from much farther away, and the styling of a person's hair gives an immediate clue as to whether they are masculine or feminine. And since it has been said that once a mental assignment of gender has been made for someone, it takes three pieces of contradictory information to change that "incorrect" gender assignment, this first impression is important.

Having good hair makes a transgender woman feel more confident because it makes "passing" so much easier.

One could assume that it would be a rare occasion for a cisgender woman to get mistaken for a man simply because she is having a bad hair day. However, recognizing that many transgender women are tall, may have angular features, probably have big hands, may have larger feet, and may not move with stereotypical feminine grace, you can see how having good hair could be quite important in tipping the scale toward the feminine.

You will notice, when looking at my photos from throughout the years, that my pictures illustrate a variety of hairstyles and colors. This is certainly not unusual, as many cisgender women change their hairstyle and color frequently as well. Unfortunately, I come from a family of women with thin, fine hair, and my mother's hair is almost as thin and fine as mine. I remember her working diligently on my grandmother's hair and putting it up in pin curls on at least a weekly basis, because she also had very thin, fine hair. And as I looked at old family photos of my great-grandmothers and even my great-great-grandmothers, I realized that the pattern of women with very thin, fine hair seems to have been a persistent theme in my family for many generations.

But the dilemma of hair goes much deeper for myself and for many transgender women.

Unfortunately, many transgender women also have the genetic predisposition for male pattern baldness. And depending upon when they begin transition, that hair loss pattern may or may not have already begun to express itself.

In my case, since I began my transition at a relatively late date—at the age of forty-five—my male pattern baldness was already fairly well advanced. That loss of hair was accentuated by the chemotherapy I had in 1998. When I went to a medical clinic for an evaluation regarding hair transplantation surgery, I asked the doctor, "What effect does chemotherapy have on male pattern baldness?" and he told me, "Chemotherapy usually causes the balding pattern to progress forward about a decade." When I asked the doctor how thick we could make the transplanted hair, he said about half as thick as the area from which it came.

I guess that's why I've always thought transplanted hair looks fine, thin, and delicate. I have only one friend that I know of who has had extensive hair transplantation, and while her hair looks nice enough for day-to-day living, it's just thin enough that it never really looks full and elegant—not like you would want to look for a festive, formal event. That less-than-perfect result, combined with a $30,000 price tag, was enough to dissuade me from having the procedure done. And believe it or not, even after having gotten the transplants, this friend still wears a wig to formal events.

I've worn various wigs and tried custom hair systems over the years. I think the best result came from the custom, full-coverage, human-hair replacement system I wore for many years. The unfortunate thing about that system, however, was that it was both expensive and required a great deal of maintenance. Since it was bonded directly to my scalp, I needed to go in about every six weeks to have the system removed, have my remaining hair colored, have the bald portion of my scalp shaved, and then have the system bonded back into place. And in addition to everything else, it made my head quite hot in the summertime.

When I moved to California and was still working for corporate America, I tolerated the expensive and inconvenient systems. It felt necessary because I had to go to work every day. I needed to look professional, and I was willing to tolerate the inconvenience for the sake of beauty.

I think the hair replacement systems became most problematic for me after Deb and I bought our boat. While we were cruising up and down the West Coast of North America, going from Canada to Mexico and back again, I stopped wearing the system and wore nothing but my natural hair for about two years. I knew that my natural hair looked acceptable, but it certainly wasn't thick and beautiful, by any stretch of the imagination! So I usually wore a hat or a visor to keep my head covered, and to avoid sunburn.

After we stopped cruising and Deb went back to work, I started experimenting with smaller, lighter versions of the hair replacement systems. These were less bulky and less inconvenient than the larger systems, but they still had the same problems of ongoing maintenance and repair. Not to mention, matching my natural hair color was becoming significantly more difficult because the sun quickly bleached and dried the systems. I also noticed that when we had boat club raft-ups with our friends I was avoiding getting into water because dealing with my hair after swimming was just too inconvenient.

This was not the way I wanted to spend my boating time, so my hairdresser and I developed a plan that would eventually allow me to do away with all the artificial systems and wear my own natural hair again. We decided to grow my bangs out, give me a permanent, and then cut and style my hair in a fairly short "A-cut" or "bob" look.

Yes, I still have very thin, very fine hair, and no, it doesn't look as full and thick and beautiful as the systems did—but it is much more comfortable, I don't have nearly as much daily maintenance as I once did, and I don't have to go in to have my hair repaired or re-bonded to my scalp. Not to mention, I don't have to avoid getting into the water like I did when I wore the systems.

And frankly, the more I look around at other women my age, the more thin, fine, and patchy hair I see. So I've got *lots* of cisgender company.

Chapter 31

"Formerly" Transsexual?
(2014)

When I first heard the phrase "formerly transsexual" many years ago, I will admit that I was both surprised and a little shocked. How in the world could someone claim to be formerly transsexual? You either are or you are not! This condition is a lifelong medical diagnosis. To me, the thought that you could ever move beyond it seemed presumptuous and arrogant.

So, here I am, living a postoperative transsexual life, fifteen years after transition and thirteen years after gender affirmation surgery—and I now completely understand the term "formerly" transsexual and, in fact, often use that descriptor to explain my current identity. Sounds ludicrous, doesn't it?

Here's the way it makes sense to me: It wasn't an overnight change, nor do I remember the day I claimed that term. It was an evolution over time, and a gradual softening of identifying with all things trans.

When I first began my transitional journey and began to recognize my true transgender nature, I became consumed with everything I could find that would help me come to terms with being trans. And looking back (as you may recall from one of my earlier writings), I was drawn to gender-variant topics like transsexuality, transvestism, and hermaphrodism at a very early age. But since I didn't identify with those terms, I didn't really do anything with the information or express myself through any transgender activity. Essentially, I lived in a state of repression or subconscious denial—though I did dress as a girl for that one Halloween as a teenager, and, as I told my mother in the letter I shared in this book, it felt "way too natural."

Because of all this, when I rediscovered these feelings at the age of forty-five, they came back to life quickly and dramatically. I was once again consumed by the interest—only this time it wasn't something I could push away!

As time went by, especially after living full-time as the woman I was intended to be, my identification with and participation in situations, activities, and friendships that revolve around everything trans began to mellow. At first, the frequency of my involvement with social activities within the trans community diminished only slightly; before too many years had passed, however, those trans-related activities were marked as being exceptions rather than the norm.

This was especially true after I moved to California and met Deb. She has always known she was a lesbian, has never been married to a man, and doesn't have any children. So living a Northern California lesbian lifestyle wasn't anything unusual for her; it was her normal way of life. Then I came along and things changed almost instantly for her.

When we met, Deb was essentially uninformed regarding the transgender community, as are many of our LGB peers. She knew we were out there, of course, and had been to enough PrideFest events to recognize that there is a wide level of diversity within the trans community, but that was about all she knew.

At the beginning of our relationship, I helped her understand the complete spectrum of being transgender, and we even attended one multi-day "California Dreaming" transgender conference together. So I guess you could say that Deb got pushed into the deep end of the transgender swimming pool. Fortunately, she's a good swimmer!

Once Deb had been adequately introduced to and educated about the T section of the LGBT community—which took about a year—we no longer felt the need to attend many trans-related events. I don't mean to minimize the importance of transgender events, as I attended many of them in my early days while exploring my own identity. But once you've fully transitioned and are in a committed relationship, the events aren't as exciting as they once were. So now we simply live our day-to-day life, pretty much like every other suburban couple.

So, what does all this have to do with being formerly trans?

As I've written about in this book, in addition to being trans, I am also a cancer survivor. I went through six months of chemotherapy and a month of radiation therapy. During that year, I was completely involved with, and consumed by, all things cancer-related. I went to appointments, studied the methodology behind my treatments and diagnosis, and went to support groups—but mostly I stayed home sick. It was a dramatic and life-changing time in my life. But I'm now completely done with it! My oncologist even used the word "cured" at the end of my ten-year check-up appointment.

So cancer was an event I transitioned through. There was a time before cancer, a time of being treated and recovering from cancer, and now there's the time after cancer. Today I am no longer a cancer patient, and I am certainly not the cancer that once defined me.

Similarly, in my day-to-day life I no longer define myself as a transsexual woman, thereby mentally separating myself from cisgender women. Being transsexual is no more a part of my current life than cancer is. I survived cancer, and I survived being transsexual. And I am now neither one of those two things. I am simply a middle-aged lesbian woman living in Northern California with a few more scars than some.

I realize this concept will be difficult for some to grasp, as it was for me when I first heard it many years ago. I am also aware that many will completely and adamantly disagree with the entire notion.

As I said at the beginning of this book, this is *my* story and *my* perspective. I do not pretend to speak for others or say that my perception is somehow superior or more truthful than the opinions and perspectives of others. We must all live our lives individually, and by definition, no two will be exactly the same.

Yes, I lived the first forty-five years of my life trying desperately to be comfortable living as a "real" man (and apparently did a relatively decent job of it). And yes, that gives me a different perspective than someone who has lived their entire life as a cisgender woman. But those differences do not in any way diminish my reality as the woman I am today. To say otherwise would infer that I am somehow still living my life fraudulently—and I assure you, I am not.

Chapter 32

The Art of "Passing"
(2015)

Nothing strikes more fear into the heart of a transgender person than the thought of going out in public for the very first time—and most of this fear comes from concerns about "passing."

Passing can be defined as a person's successful and unquestioned movement through society as the gender for which they are currently dressed. In other words, if you were assigned the gender of male on your birth certificate and have been living and dressing as male most of your life, when you go out in public dressed as female for the first time, you're desperately hoping nobody will notice! And if nobody does notice, then you're passing.

Unfortunately, the act of successfully passing is a very complex issue.

When I was preparing for my very first night out dressed as a woman, I had done a great deal of preliminary homework. I had gone to the Gender Identity Center for some helpful hints about where to safely shop for shoes, clothes, undergarments, hair, and makeup. And I had taken that knowledge even further by making an appointment at a local "gender boutique" for my initial makeover. As mentioned in an earlier chapter, prior to that appointment, I had already done my shopping, so all I needed to do was show up at the salon with my suitcase full of the essentials, and let them work their magic.

But just because I'd had my hair and makeup professionally done didn't necessarily mean that I would pass as female when venturing out in public.

Fortunately for me, on that first evening of dressing as a woman, I was driving straight from the salon to the Gender Identity Center for their weekly meeting, and after the meeting my friends and I were going out as a group to a local gay bar where there was a weekly drag show. So we really weren't spending any significant time in the "straight world." That made my introduction into public society much safer and more comfortable.

The nearly instantaneous mental assignment of gender, which we all engage in, is based on a number of things. First and foremost are the clothes and hair. This is followed immediately by a quick visual scan of the shape of the face, brow, throat, shoulders, breasts, and right on down the rest of the body. This scan is also when we pick up on any subtle energetic clues, such as insecurity, embarrassment, or lack of confidence. Needless to say, few transgender people can truly say they were confident on their very first time out in public.

Then there is the evaluation regarding size of feet, hands, and ease of movement. Men and women move quite differently, so unless a trans woman has spent time walking, sitting, standing, and practicing various movements in their new attire before going out in public, they're likely going to be immediately identified as "a man in a dress." This is the opposite of passing and is called being "read"—and nothing could be more horrifying to the neophyte transgender woman! Being "read" is akin to ultimate failure in presenting as a woman, and is usually accompanied by shame, embarrassment, fear, and a host of other negative emotions. Depending on the situation and location, being read can also sometimes be physically dangerous.

Personally, I did spend a fair amount of time practicing at home while wearing my heels and skirt. Lucky for me, at that time, I had the support of my then-wife. That practice allowed me to move with at least a modicum of grace so I wouldn't be quite as awkward in public, and hopefully wouldn't draw unwanted attention.

Inconsistencies in overall presentation are what will get you read. As a trans woman, you can move with the ease and grace of a ballerina, but if your voice is deep and masculine, as soon as you speak, you'll be read. You can be small in stature and have flawless hair and makeup, but if you walk like a lumberjack, you'll be read. It's about consistency and an overall feminine presentation.

Of course, the reverse is true for female to male transsexuals. Transsexual men have the issue of typically being shorter and smaller than most cisgender men. Their hands and feet are also smaller, and early in transition their voices are higher. But once they start taking testosterone, their voice changes fairly quickly, they begin to grow facial hair, and if male pattern baldness runs in the family, their hairline begins to recede. Those obvious changes quickly overshadow the fact that they are smaller than most cisgender men.

Overall, I believe early-transitioning trans men have an easier time passing than do the rest of us in the trans community, because the societal expectations of gender expression for women are much more narrow. But since my personal experience is with a male-to-female transition, I'll restrict most of my comments to things of which I have firsthand knowledge.

Unless a transgender woman transitions before the onset of male puberty and takes puberty-blocking hormones, there are substantial physical changes that she must overcome in order to consistently pass. The most obvious example is the Adam's apple. The Adam's apple is a prominent enlargement of the larynx (voice box) that occurs to support the thickening of the vocal chords as the voice deepens during male puberty. This cartilage can be surgically removed, but that procedure is not without danger. When I had my tracheal shave, my voice actually got lower after the procedure. This was certainly not what I wanted! Fortunately, as the months went by, and with consistent vocal training, I managed to get my voice back up to my pre-surgical tone. Being a singer definitely helped in this regard.

Other fixed biological issues are more difficult, if not impossible, to change. Things such as larger hands and feet are completely permanent and unchangeable. Men also generally have broader shoulders, bigger muscles, and thicker bones, and on average, they are several inches taller than women. So the late-transitioning transgender woman comes into her post-puberty transition with the deck already stacked against her passing as cisgender. Facial characteristics such as sharp facial angles, strong brow bones, and a prominent lower jaw, however, can be successfully modified with facial feminization surgery (FFS).

I am five foot nine inches tall. This is just about average for a male of my age, but quite tall for a woman of my generation. When I was living as a man, nobody ever commented on my height. But once I started living as a woman, I was often asked if I was a model, and people frequently commented on my being very tall. It's all in the perception of "normal."

Voice training is a common and necessary step in transition. This training might take place in a formal setting with a transgender voice coach, or it may be informal, done at home with online resources, or simply by studying the differences between how men and women speak. There's the obvious difference in tone, but as I mentioned in an earlier chapter, that difference is typically only about the equivalent of three musical notes. And there are many women with deep voices that would never be taken for male. (Kathleen Turner is a perfect example of this.) With practice, I believe nearly anyone can raise the tone of their speaking voice by those three notes. But the biggest differences come with word usage and inflection.

Men speak with a tonal range that tends to remain flat or go down at the end of a sentence. Women have more variation in tone within their phraseology and typically end sentences with a lifting tone, almost like they're asking a question. These changes can be learned, but it takes lots of practice. When I was working on my voice, I would intentionally exaggerate these differences, especially while speaking on the phone, in order to not be called "sir" by the person on the other end of the line. In fact, my former girlfriend Cristina, the woman I was living with during most of my transition, would often tease me when I hung up the phone, asking, "Who was that girly-girl talking on the phone?" I always considered it a wonderful day when I could "pass," even on the telephone.

The number of transgender women who simply will not work on this all-important issue surprises me. I've occasionally heard transgender women complain about their inability to pass, all the while speaking in a voice that is obviously masculine. Unfortunately, without a consistently feminine speaking voice, passing will always remain a problem. For some trans women, I think the unwillingness to work on their voice stems from a belief that it will be impossible for them to sound feminine simply because they have such a naturally low voice. Or, in some cases, trans women may be so physically large that they could never pass as cisgender regardless of their voice, so they adopt a "why bother" attitude. However, with proper coaching and a lot of practice, anyone can learn to speak with a feminine voice. My pre-transition voice was so low that I sang bass or baritone in a men's quartet.

About three years into transition, I ran across an old frequent-flier account that had not yet been transferred into my new name. I was hoping I could just make a quick call and change the name over the phone. The agent was friendly enough about changing the name but was obviously confused about why she was now speaking to a woman instead of the man whose name was on the account.

Because this was many years ago, and because I didn't want to go through my entire medical history with her over the phone, I used the sometimes-convenient excuse of, "This account change is due to a divorce settlement." She remained friendly and simply stated, "Dr. Tomlinson will need to call us and give us permission to change the name on the account." Without missing a beat, I answered, "Well this is our lucky day, because it just so happens that he's here right now picking up some papers." I set the phone down and called out, "Allen, could you come to the phone for a minute?" Then I picked up the phone and said in my old baritone male voice, "This is Allen Tomlinson, how can I help you?"

At that point, the agent simply asked for permission to change the name and I granted it, and that was the end of the conversation. So the old voice is definitely still there if ever needed. It's all about training and practice.

Perhaps this was a cowardly way out, and yes, I know, I missed an opportunity to educate yet another customer support person over the phone about transgender issues, but sometimes I just got tired of repeating the same story over and over. Not to mention, once that transgender door has been opened, they often then require *all* the supporting documentation to make the requested changes. And that is a pain in the butt.

Another important part of passing concerns this indefinable and nebulous thing called energy. We can all sense energy from those around us, and yet it is a feeling that is nearly impossible to quantify. Some people say this "something" comes from our very essence, moves up through our chakras, and radiates out through our aura. Certainly there is a difference between masculine and feminine energy.

The more time a transgender woman spends cultivating this desired feminine energy, and the more time she's spent living as a woman (and socializing with other women), the more this energy will simply radiate from her. This is especially true after going on hormone therapy.

In summary, for trans women, the ability to pass comes down to consistency in presenting yourself as having what are typically considered "feminine" characteristics. The secret is remaining constant with energy, appearance, movement, and voice. If you're consistent with those, the other physical detractors won't even matter.

★ ★ ★

I am writing this book as a source of inspiration and education for those interested in transsexuality. Part of our societal education comes from the evolution of language. When I began my transition many years ago, I would never have even questioned the pejorative implied meaning of the term "passing." Now that I am many years on the "other side" of transition, however, I see things much differently.

To some people, the word "passing" implies that there is something deceptive going on. It says there is something disingenuous or artificial, in a trans woman's successful presentation as female. If you pass, then nobody really knows the "real" you. So essentially, if you pass, you are deceiving those around you.

Perpetuating the idea of passing also supports the gender binary. That binary point of view incorrectly states that all people are either 100 percent male or 100 percent female and that there can be no blending of the two or moving in and out of androgyny. Biological variation is seldom that unequivocal.

Simply stated, these binary positions are false constructions. People who are transgender are not trying to deceive anyone! We're simply trying to live our lives in an authentic manner that keeps us safe, happy, and feeling fulfilled as a person. We may or may not live within the societal gender binary, but there is absolutely nothing deceptive in either path. The only real deception that I've practiced in my life occurred when I was acting the part of someone whom I was not. My journey through transition was an outward expression of who I truly am inside, and there can be no hidden agenda in the authentic expression of Self.

Chapter 33

Hormones
(2015)

The changes that occur when a transsexual woman goes on hormone replacement therapy (HRT) are nothing short of remarkable. Not only does the therapy change your body, it changes your mind and emotional range, and creates an entirely new worldview.

From my earliest outings as a gender dysphoric cross-dresser, there was always a distinct difference between the appearance, actions, and feminine energy of those who were merely cross-dressing versus those who were in transition or seriously contemplating transition. Women who were transitioning did not necessarily need to be on hormones in order for some of these differences to be apparent, but if they were already on HRT, the distinction was striking. These were no longer men attempting, in varying degrees, to pass as female—they simply *were* women! And it had absolutely nothing to do with their clothing. In fact, most transitioning women dressed quite conservatively compared to the rest of the drag and/or cross-dressing community.

Because I felt, at a deep, intuitive level, from my very first night as Alexandra that my feminine self was my authentic self,

I was always interested in socializing with, and being a part of, the transsexual subgroup of the transgender community. I felt like this was where I most easily fit in, even though at first I was trying desperately to be just a crossdresser. I would try to hang out with the cross-dressing group, but usually found the conversation uninteresting. I guess at some subconscious level I knew I'd be transitioning myself someday, so I always gravitated toward the transsexual women.

People who are contemplating transition often ask if there is an optimal time to start hormone therapy. The usual answer is, "As soon as possible." It takes years for the hormones to have the completely desired result, and you have to go through a second puberty once they begin to take effect, so three to five years is typical.

For those who aren't sure if they're actually transsexual or not, being on hormones for a month will most definitely answer that question. Either the hormones will have a calming and life-expanding effect, or they'll be frightening and simply feel wrong. If the effect feels wrong, you can simply stop taking the hormones and things will revert back to the way they were before in just a few days. (Note: This is not to be taken as medical advice and you should never start cross-gender hormone therapy without a doctor's prescription.)

My personal experience was that even the natural amount of male testosterone my body produced made me aggressive, competitive, and oversexed. My emotional range consisted of three speeds: normal, happy, or angry. I really didn't experience much of an emotional spectrum outside those three feelings.

When I started on estrogen, it was as if someone had taken off the blinders I had unknowingly worn for my entire life. The world was suddenly made up of a spectrum of wonderful emotions and feelings I had never before experienced. I went from those three basic emotional speeds to an infinite range of feelings that I didn't even know existed. It was like experiencing life as simply vanilla, strawberry, or chocolate, and then suddenly being able to taste thirty-one flavors or more! I felt like I was Dorothy in *The Wizard of Oz* when she goes from living the black-and-white version of Kansas to the Technicolor experiences of Oz. It really was that dramatic!

Once I started on hormones, there was never even a consideration of whether or not I was on the right path. I absolutely knew I was going where I needed to go. It was as if my body was saying, "It's about time! What took you so long?"

Not only was my emotional spectrum infinitely multiplied, my view of the entire world changed dramatically. I now saw the world through a completely new set of lenses, much like a professional photographer might use different lenses to set the mood of the photo they are about to take. Everything I saw and felt was expanded, softer, more detailed, full of nuance, and had an infinite number of descriptors and feelings within. Questions and answers about life were no longer simply yes or no, good or bad, right or wrong, black or white. Instead, there were an infinite number of answers within all those questions. Testosterone versus estrogen isn't just about Mars versus Venus, it's like comparing different galaxies.

Now that I've been post-transition for over fifteen years, and am currently in the early senior citizen range of womanhood, I no longer need to take hormones. And no, my body will not revert back to masculine; there's no significant testosterone to cause that to happen. Instead, I will age and experience the rest of life just like any other post-menopausal woman.

Chapter 34

Nikki's Story: My Dad is a Transgender Lesbian
(2016)

As I sat down to write this chapter on my perspective of Alexus's transition I realized it's something I've been putting off for fifteen years. Wow. That's an embarrassing thing to realize and admit. FIFTEEN YEARS. Is that even possible? It begs the question, why? Why have I been putting off doing something that I WANT to do? For someone I love? My sister wrote one many years ago. And she had a much harder time with the transition than I did. Yet she still managed to sit down and write her story. Why didn't I? I've always been a good student. I got straight A's through school and was valedictorian of my high school class. I've always followed direction well. I've always been a pleaser and a perfectionist. So what's the hangup here? I've been through lots of therapy and consider myself a well-adjusted, emotionally evolved person. So why have I ignored sharing my perspective of this unique situation with the world? I can *talk* to people about it. Sure. I have no trouble *telling* folks the story and how I feel about everything. Conversations? No problem. But writing it down . . . Now that's a different story. It feels more concrete. Like my words are somehow etched in stone. Like it has to be done perfectly, because there's no going back.

I guess you could say I've had a fifteen-year case of writer's block on the issue. I think that's because I truly I want to tell the story right. I want to do it justice. Alexus is one of the bravest, most inspiring, smart, amazing, caring, honest, exceptional people I know. And I want my piece in the story to be right. To be accurate. To be meaningful. To be honest. So I guess that's all I have to do. Be honest. Tell my story from my perspective, the way I see it. There actually is no right. There's only my version. So that's what I will attempt to do. Share with you all how I see it. How I feel it. How it affects me.

I guess I'll start from the beginning. Allen. He was my dad. He was a great dad, and a not-so-great dad. Great in that he always pushed me to excel. To try something new. To learn about the world. To be the best. I'm absolutely the perfectionist I am today because of Allen's pushing. He was into SCUBA diving, so I got my SCUBA certification when I was just twelve years old. That's the youngest you can be and still get certified. And I'd have done it when I was eight if they'd have let me.

He was an adventure seeker, too. We took family vacations to Hawaii and walked around the volcanoes where the lava was actively flowing (which was definitely NOT allowed, but we crossed the ropes anyway to get a close-up look at the marvels of nature). We went parasailing. He was a pilot, so we'd rent airplanes and go up on flights into the mountains. He raced bicycles. We swam with dolphins. We went on manta ray dives. He took a special dental class at the Pankey Institute in Florida, where they were dissecting halves of human cadaver heads, and I got to go in and see them and get a close-up look. I learned a lot from my dad. I was a smart little girl because of him.

I also learned that perfection is the only thing that matters. That being the best is the only way to be valuable. Allen was not a

Nikki's Story: My Dad is a Transgender Lesbian

very happy guy. In fact, I think he was downright miserable most of the time. Which I think explains all the adventure seeking. He was desperately looking for something to fill that hole in his soul, that giant void within him that indicated something was wrong. He was an adrenaline junkie. When the adrenaline was flowing, he felt happy. Fulfilled. But as any junkie knows, the highs are short-lived. Then the crash back down to earth and reality happens. You're back where you were. Miserable for no good reason. Allen was angry. He was impatient. He could be downright scary at times. One of my most profound therapy moments happened when my therapist and I discovered that throughout my young life I was legitimately afraid that my dad would kill me. I have very distinct, specific memories of moments when I thought that might happen. I can pinpoint them. I was terrified. I lived in survival mode a lot of the time. He and my mom would fight. Their relationship was not healthy. At least it didn't seem like it to me. And I was always on my mom's side. She was loving. Caring. Tender. Gentle. Understanding.

I can remember one moment when I was in the fifth grade, sitting in the kitchen of our rented duplex in Denver, crying with my mom and sister because my parents had just had a terrible fight and I thought they were going to get divorced. I remember thinking, *If I never see my dad again in my whole life, that will be fine. He can just walk right out the door right now and never come back. And we'll be better for it. If he gets killed, oh well. I don't ever want to see him again anyway.* So yeah. As I said, great and not so great.

The first inkling of Alexus's transition happened for me quite by accident. I was upstairs in my dad's office, where the only computer in the house was. Where he spent most of his time. Isolated. Away from the rest of the family. (That was a point of contention between my parents.)

I was playing a computer game. I needed paper or something. So I went looking through the desk drawers and cabinets, digging, looking for whatever it was I needed. What I found was entirely unexpected. I found glamorous photos of a woman. This woman was beautiful. She had fancy hair and makeup. Beautiful beaded gowns on. Some photos in a red business suit. Some of the other photos were sexy and provocative; she was in lingerie.

This woman was gorgeous. And she was NOT my mom. My initial thought was, *Oh my gosh, my dad is having an affair. This explains so much.* I had had conversations with my mom where I would ask her what was wrong, and fighting back the tears she would say, "Something is going on with your dad. Something bad. Beyond what you can possibly even imagine." My young brain didn't know what to make of that. But now, all of a sudden, things seemed to make sense. My dad was cheating on my mom.

But as I sat, devastated, looking at the photos, I slowly started to realize something . . . *Wait a minute . . . This is not another woman. THIS IS MY DAD.*

Whoa. Mind blown. I looked closer. Was it? Could it possibly be? Yes. It definitely was. There was no mistaking. The photos were of my dad dressed up as a woman. A beautiful woman, posing for pictures.

I put them away. I didn't know what to think about it or how to feel. I knew I shouldn't have found them. I shouldn't have seen them. That was clear. I wouldn't tell anyone else about this. And I have kept that secret until this very writing.

I was officially told by my parents sometime after that. They sat me down, family meeting–style, and said they needed to talk to me about something. I was nervous. My little sister wasn't present, it was just me. They said, "You know how you like to get dressed up gothic sometimes and go have coffee with Teresa?"

(Side note: I was a very white bread, goodie-two-shoes, blond, straight A's, show choir, cheerleader sort. And occasionally my friend Teresa and I used to get dressed up full Goth—white faces, black makeup, black clothes, big combat boots, fake piercings, the whole nine yards—and go have coffee dressed like that. There were a couple different coffee shops in town known for being frequented by the Goth crowd on certain nights, so we'd usually go to one of those. We enjoyed dressing up as characters totally outside our "normal" realm and soaking up all the looks we'd get as we drove there and walked from place to place from both the Goth and the non-Goth folks. We liked the attention. We liked playing totally different characters. We had fun.)

So my parents said, "You know how you sometimes like to get dressed up Gothic and go have coffee with Teresa? Well, your dad does something similar. He sometimes likes to get dressed up as a woman and go out in drag."

Cool! I thought. *My dad is significantly cooler than I thought he was!* He instantly went up a couple rungs on the coolness ladder. I'd always thought we had sort of a boring family, and now, suddenly, here was something interesting!

"Okay," I said, and wanted to know more. They told me how his drag name was Alexandra and how sometimes she would sing and perform in the drag clubs. I think they were afraid that I might be out some time with my musical theater friends and accidentally end up at a drag show where this all-too-familiar drag queen named Alexandra was performing. They didn't want me to discover it that way. They wanted to be the ones to tell me.

Little did they know I'd already discovered the secret. But now I knew what those pictures meant. They were nothing to worry about! It was just my dad having fun. There was no affair going on, he wasn't cheating on my mom, he was just getting dressed up as a woman—a hot, sexy woman—and going out on the town performing. Awesome. Nothing wrong with that in my book.

As the months progressed, the dressing in drag continued. At some point my parents decided to tell Erika, my little sister. It was decided that it would be best to keep it a family secret and not let other people know, as Erika was in middle school at the time and was quite the popular social butterfly. No one wanted her social status or reputation tarnished, especially since middle school can be quite tough as it is. So a family secret it would be. At the time it seemed like the best, most thought-out, respectful, compassionate plan. Looking back now, in hindsight, I can see that keeping it a secret inadvertently communicated to my sister that it was something to be ashamed of. Something embarrassing that needed to be hidden and kept from the world. I regret that. I wish we had been able to do better for her. But all you can do in any given moment is the best you can do at the time. And that's what we did.

So Alexandra continued to dress and go out. It started as only dressing in drag and going out to sing in the drag shows. Then it was dressing and going out to the gay bar, even when she wasn't performing. Then dressing and going out to an after-hours straight club. Then dressing and going out to a regular bar. Then dressing and going out to dinner. Then dressing and going out in the afternoon to the mall or a movie. The dressing became more and more frequent and less and less flamboyant. She was slowly realizing that she was not a drag queen or a crossdresser, but rather was leaning toward being transgender. Alexus was beginning to emerge.

I must pause the transition story at this time to interject a paragraph about cancer. Allen had been diagnosed with Hodgkin's lymphoma. Late stage 3, significant cancer of the lymph system. He had hundreds of nodes all throughout his lymph system and a massive tumor that took up over a third of his chest cavity. It was bad. He was to start chemotherapy and radiation right away. It was a shock. It was scary. I remember telling my best friend at the time, Stacey, about the diagnosis. We cried. She felt sorry for me. And I remember thinking, *There's also this other huge secret, but I can't tell you about that.*

As Allen was going through chemo and radiation, I was looking at universities and deciding what college I wanted to attend. I remember going to visit the College of Santa Fe and her hair (wow, here's where pronouns obviously start to get tricky for me; Alexus was in the very early stages of transitioning at this time, so when I look back on the story it feels sort of natural for me to call her "her" during this stage, even though she was not at all living full-time as a woman yet. She was still very much Allen, living with cancer, who MIGHT be in the early stages of transitioning. I find it interesting that my brain starts to muddy the pronouns at this point). Anyway . . . his/her hair was falling out. We were visiting the College of Santa Fe and it was embarrassing and sort of gross to constantly look over and see big chunks of hair falling out and sitting on his shoulder or falling down the front of his shirt. "Dad, you have a bunch of hair on you," I remember saying while sitting at a restaurant in downtown Santa Fe.

It's a weird thing to watch one of your parents pull fistfuls of hair out of their head at a restaurant. I had a sick feeling in my stomach about it all. It was sad, gross, and real life. When we got home from the trip my parents decided to shave my dad's head so the hair falling out wouldn't be an issue. It was strange, but was going to be for the best.

He looked weird with no hair. Wigs started to enter the scene.

As the cancer treatments continued, my dad found a book. It was by a woman named Louise Hay and was called *You Can Heal Your Life*. This book would change her life. And my life. It has since become my personal bible of sorts. Louise Hay's whole philosophy in this book is that physical diseases, illnesses, injuries, etc. are simply an outward, physical manifestation of troublesome inner issues and negative thought patterns. They manifest physically in a dis-ease of the body. A disease. I jive with that. At the back of the book Louise has a whole section that lists different diseases, illnesses, and injuries and charts what the negative thought pattern could be that's causing the issue, then a new, positive thought pattern or affirmation that can be repeated to change it and heal yourself. Hence the title of the book, *You Can Heal Your Life*.

In this section, Alexus (Allen at the time) found the Hodgkin's disease line. The negative thought pattern or probable cause was all to do with pleasing other people and not being genuine. Not being enough. A frantic race for acceptance. She said reading that section took her breath away and she felt like someone had hit her in the chest with a 2x4. It was accurate. Dead accurate. And she realized if she didn't change something, she would quite literally die. It was indeed a matter of life and death.

The new thought pattern to repeat and begin implementing was, "I am perfectly happy to be me. I am good enough just as I am. I love and approve of myself. I am joy expressing and receiving." Holy yikes. She had to be her. A genuine, authentic expression of her true self. And that was starting to look like being a woman. Terrifying. Especially for a white, upper-middle-class man. Conservative. Husband. Father of two children. Dentist. Son of ultraconservative, farmer parents from rural Kansas. I can't even imagine. But the change had to happen. She knew not making the change was a death sentence. Talk about being stuck between a rock and hard place.

As Alexus began to transition she started asking me for advice on all things female. Makeup tips, hair tricks, fashion advice, etc. It was weird at times to be giving my dad that sort of advice. But I also found it fun. It was an entirely new kind of father-daughter bonding. And for the first time this bonding felt genuine. I wasn't afraid of making a mistake or messing up. She was coming to me as a vulnerable, real person who genuinely needed advice and help from her daughter. And I was happy to give it. She was starting to transition into being a woman. And I could see her changing. I could see the unhappiness releasing and going away. She was becoming warm. Compassionate. I saw her cry out of sympathy for me and other creatures. She was becoming tender. Empathetic. I liked this new person I saw emerging. To throw a couple clichés in, it was like his cold heart was melting away and hers was developing. Or like when the Grinch's heart grew three sizes that day. That's what I saw occurring.

I know this time was rough for my mom and my sister. They were having a much harder time with the transition than I was. Which is certainly understandable. I had many lengthy conversations with each of them about it. My mom felt like Alexus was being selfish. "How dare s/he rip our family apart this way." My sister thought it was weird and gross and embarrassing. "I can't believe my dad is doing this. Don't let anyone see you when you come to pick me up from dance class." I felt bad for each of them. I could honestly see where they were both coming from and I tried my best to help them see my perspective on it. But they weren't ready for that. They each needed to grieve and be angry and experience all the emotions they felt about it at the time. And that was fine. It had to be.

One of the most difficult parts of Alexus's transition for me was watching how it affected my mom. It did tear her apart. It ripped the rug right out from under her. And I felt bad for her. When Alexandra was still on the scene and still in the phase of going out in extravagant drag outfits and lavish makeup and hair, my mom was really trying to hang in there, be strong and supportive, and do what was best for the family. (She is an amazing woman.) She would go out with Alexandra and her drag friends. My mom was the only cisgender woman there, and she was completely overlooked. In the shadow of the drag queens, one of whom happened to be her husband. I can't imagine how hard and painful that must have been for her.

To combat this, she decided to redo portions of herself as well. She had breast implants and liposuction. They were things she had always wanted to do. But now, it seemed to me, they came from a desire to keep up. It was hard to watch her go through that. Both the emotional piece and the physical piece. That's a lot to have done all in one surgery. The recovery was painful. The medication made her emotional and she cried a lot. She couldn't raise her arms above her head to brush her hair. Other elements of the recovery made her extremely vulnerable. She was helpless. She was no longer the pillar of strength and support I had come to rely on. It was uncomfortable for me to be around and painful to watch. Both of my parents were literally changing right in front of me.

Once my mom recovered and Alexus identified that a full transition with surgery was where she was headed, they decided to split. Alexus was becoming a woman, and my mom is not a lesbian. This marriage was no longer going to work. I was out working on a cruise ship at the time the divorce news rolled in, and I was happy about it, yet felt a bit sad at the same time. I knew the divorce was going to allow each of my parents to be more happy apart than they were together.

Alexus moved out of our house and into a condo nearby. When I returned home from my work stint, it was strange to not have her in the house, but good that she now had her own place close by. She was also getting much closer to having her reassignment surgery. I went over to her condo one day and said, "Okay, people are going to ask me about this and I'll need to know. How is this surgery done? What do they actually do? Does it look real?"

She seemed surprised by my questions, but was willing to answer them. We sat down at her computer and she began by explaining that vaginas are all very different. Even cisgender women's vaginas are all quite different and can vary a lot. So we looked at pictures. We saw that the clitoris can be all different sizes and in different places (relatively speaking). The inner and outer labia are all totally different. Then she pulled up two pictures of vaginas, one belonging to a cisgender woman and one belonging to a transgender woman. She asked if I could identify which was which. I couldn't. I had no idea. *Wow*, I thought, *they really do look real!*

She then explained and found photos and diagrams of how the male-to-female surgery is actually done. How the penis is basically inverted and repurposed to create a nearly full-functioning vagina and clitoris. I was amazed! This was definitely an unusual father-daughter conversation, but one I respected immensely and was grateful for. Her ability to be open and honest throughout the entire process meant a lot. It helped me to feel comfortable. I could always ask her any questions I had, and she was always willing to answer them and talk openly about any aspect of her transition. It helped me learn a lot about it all, and also helped me understand what was happening. I could then explain it to other people who had never had any contact with anyone transgender before. I enjoyed helping people see how "normal" it all really is. And that I am normal (well, relatively speaking, haha). And that Alexus is a wonderful, caring, smart, funny human being.

When people say, "Oh man, I've got a crazy family," I've usually got them beat. Saying, "My dad is a transgender lesbian" pretty much tops anyone else's "crazy." And I couldn't be more grateful for it.

Alexus is now remarried to an amazing woman named Debbie. My sister and I stood up in the wedding and I sang a couple of songs during the ceremony. It was lovely. I also did Alexus's makeup for the big day. They are living happily as lesbians in Northern California.

Alexus living her genuine, authentic self allowed her to get out of the race for acceptance and just be her. I've learned from her that there is no such thing as perfect. The only right is what's right for you. I still struggle a bit with the compulsion to be perfect, hence my fifteen-year procrastination writing this piece. But it's all a work in progress. I'm a work in progress. And I'm glad Alexus was brave enough to live out her full expression of authentic self and model that for me. She's pretty perfect in my eyes. I now know that true value and self-worth comes not from being the best but from being the best you. We're all different. Unique. Special. Worthy. And I think it's about time we all start acknowledging that and appreciating the differences and worthiness in both ourselves and others.

Thank you, Alexus, for everything you've taught me by being you.

Chapter 35

From Puberty to Senior Citizen in Only Eighteen Years
(2016)

When a transgender person starts taking cross-gender hormones they go through a second puberty. The body begins to transform, the mind begins to rewire, and emotions expand into realms of expression never before experienced. It's like being a teenager all over again. The only problem with this is, since we're now in adult bodies, this teenage-like expression can sometimes appear completely inappropriate.

I believe this is one of the reasons why some early-transition trans women are often seen dressing in the clothing styles of someone much younger. It was certainly true for me, and I also saw it in many of my friends. Since I didn't begin my transition until I was forty-seven years old, I missed several decades of fashion expression. And while being transsexual is certainly not just about the clothes, I believe most women (cisgender and trans) would say that clothing is an essential part of feminine expression.

So a middle-aged trans woman has lots of catching up to do! Looking back at some of my early pictures, I am grateful that my period of age-inappropriate dress was relatively brief. With the exception of Halloween or other costume parties or special events, I never really dressed overly provocatively, though I did occasionally wear skirts or dresses that were probably too short for a woman of my age.

As I mentioned in the chapter on hormones, my changes in thinking and expression of emotion during my transition were equally dramatic. When I first started taking estrogen, I could easily cry over something as silly as a television commercial. While this was certainly a new experience for me, it was also a comforting release of many decades of pent-up emotion. So I enjoyed crying and learned to freely express that newfound sensation. Being overly emotional is a characteristic also occasionally seen in teenage girls, as well as some cisgender women when they are nearing their monthly period. So dramatic hormonal changes most certainly aren't limited exclusively to transgender women.

About two or three years into hormone therapy, things began to stabilize. I would equate this relative emotional stability and resultant expression of feelings as what I would routinely observe in other women who were thirty-something. After experiencing the significant roller coaster ride of cross-hormonal puberty for several years, this leveling out of emotions was both welcome and fulfilling.

This seemed to manifest in both fashion and routine life. For me, this might also have been more noticeable because after my divorce and throughout most of my transition, I was in a five-year relationship with Cristina, who was in her early thirties at the time we became a couple.

Since we were also raising her young daughter, Emily, together, most of our social activities were with either other cisgender women in their thirties or my trans friends who were also early in transition. So for me, I was experiencing the equivalent of an early-adult, stay-at-home mom part of my life.

When Emily was in kindergarten, Cristina was working full-time, so I walked Emily to the school bus in the morning and I was there to walk her home when the bus arrived in early afternoon. I'd make her a snack while she watched cartoons and then she'd go outside to play with her friends or have them over to play in her room.

After my relationship with Cristina ended, I moved into a condo in another Denver suburb and continued my life as a single woman working a full-time job as a courier to pay the bills.

Since the breakup was emotionally traumatic for me, I made the conscious decision not to date anyone for at least a year; I wanted to learn who I was as a person outside of a relationship. Since I had been either married or in a committed relationship full-time since the age of nineteen, I didn't really know myself. This was exaggerated by the fact that in the previous few years, I had survived cancer, gotten divorced, and transitioned from male to female. Now, living alone as a single, fifty-something, divorced woman, I felt alone, sad, and completely adrift.

It was time to grow up and figure out who I really was.

Fortunately, driving full-time as a courier gave me lots of alone time for introspection. I listened to a lot of self-help and metaphysical audiobooks during that time. It was a yearlong period of spiritual and emotional development. My identity as a woman was also maturing, and I began to feel more like a middle-aged woman.

One day about a year after my breakup, I serendipitously met a man at my local auto shop while having the oil changed in my car. While we were waiting for our cars, we had a great conversation. He told me that he worked for a national company selling corporate communication systems and said, based on my outgoing personality and ease striking up a conversation with a complete stranger, that I'd be great at his job. The problem was that the only current job opening in the entire company was in San Jose, California.

He connected me with his boss, I sent them my resume, we did a long telephone interview, and I was hired the very next week. With only one small catch: I had to be in San Jose in two weeks. In other words, I had just two weeks to get my condo listed with a property manager, figure out how to get all my stuff moved, and start a new life in a new apartment in a new city and state with a new job. But that's also one of the ways you know when you're on your correct path: things fall into place.

As it turned out, the position in San Jose was open because the lady who had previously worked the territory was moving to Los Angeles to take over a vacant territory there. She had a furnished apartment already leased in downtown San Jose and was delighted to sublet it to me.

Meanwhile, my Denver realtor connected me with a reputable property manager, so that was done almost overnight too.

With a little research, I found a national moving company called "Pods" that brings a container to your driveway, then takes it to a warehouse after you fill it up with all your belongings and keeps it there until you're ready to have it shipped somewhere else. What could be easier?

So, less than two weeks later, I was in my little VW Golf towing a very small U-Haul trailer containing my clothes, computer, and a few other personal belongings, heading west to sunny California. When it's supposed to happen, it just happens.

This was a time when I was completely free to reinvent myself. So I became a single, fifty-something professional urban woman. There was no longer any reason to pretend to be anything other than who I was. It was quite liberating!

Once I met Deb, just a few months after moving to California, I got the opportunity to settle in and be just plain me. Of course, I still had to work, and being in a sales position keeps you "up and on stage" in order to sell the product and pay the bills—but that only continued for about a year more.

By the time Debbie and I got married, I had retired, we had bought our boat, and I was beginning to enjoy just "being." This process of trying to stay in the moment was continued and refined throughout our two years of cruising up and down the West Coast. Here, again, there was no reason to be anything other than the woman I was, and by then I was in my upper fifties.

I celebrated my sixtieth birthday shortly after we stopped cruising and were about to move back into our house in Pleasanton. I say "celebrated" because that's what you're supposed to do for your birthday. But I must confess, that birthday hit me particularly hard. I still don't understand what's so significant about the number sixty, but there was something deep inside me that changed. Somehow I felt that I was suddenly and officially "old." I was (and still am) in good health, and I continue to be active. But I guess you can't pretend to still be young and carry an AARP card. So I guess I'll just have to settle for being young at heart.

I think part of the reason turning sixty hit me so hard might be that I had just started living my truth in my early fifties. And even though I was physically "fifty-something," I felt like a young woman (because hormonally, I was). So when that decade very quickly passed and I officially moved into my sixtieth decade, I think at some level I felt cheated. I had waited so long to discover who I truly am and was just really beginning to enjoy life. And now, suddenly, society was going to see me as an old woman. I really wasn't ready for that just yet!

We now live in a 55+ community in Rio Vista, California, so we're close to our boat and are officially residents of the California Delta. Our community is technically a retirement community, and you must prove your age at multiple points throughout the process of buying a house here. Deb is still working, but I'm officially retired.

On my next birthday, I'll be eligible for Medicare, so you can easily figure out how old I'll be. And I guess that officially makes me a senior citizen. So when I go back and do the math, I started my transition and began my second puberty at age forty-seven—and now, nearly eighteen years later, I am officially a senior citizen. It's been a fast eighteen years, and I'm certainly not done yet.

It's been a very wild ride . . .

Epilogue

Random Spiritual Musings

This is a collection of random thoughts and quotes that may be helpful to others who are seeking their own individual journey through this interesting and amazing thing called life. Most are a combination of thoughts and ideas gathered from decades of personal recovery and metaphysical study.

- Spirit does not make junk.

- The Universe is very persistent.

- Everyone has a unique gift that, when fully expressed, will positively impact the world.

- No two gifts are exactly alike. There may be similarities, but your gifts cannot be the same as another person's.

- Trying to emulate another person limits authentic self-expression.

- Look within for your guidance. Others can share their perspective based on their life experience and worldview, but they can never give advice that is somehow "ultimately true" for your unique situation. Only you know the answers.

* Truly being "you" is always scary at first, because there are no exact models for your unique path.

* Society does not like people who dare to express their uniqueness, so be ready for resistance. But know that moving through the resistance will strengthen the impact of your gift.

* Resistance from society is frequently a sign that you're on the right track.

* Expressing your gift threatens the status quo.

* When you truly follow your heart, the Universe will support you—but this support may not come from those who have been important to you in the past.

* Growth will cause new people to enter your life, and those people may replace some of the people that have been previously significant.

* If life is a constant struggle, you are out of synch with your gift. Expressing your gift returns passion to your life. Living a passionate life leads to ecstasy.

* Times of ecstasy will be followed by yet another lesson. These lessons will cause further emotion. This roller coaster ride is not optional; only

the relative levels of peaks and valleys can be tempered through wisdom and enlightenment.

* If you close the door to any opportunity because of fear, you will also limit the boundless nature of the Universe.

* Choosing to ignore your inner guidance will only extend a period of discontent, it will not change the essence of the lesson to be learned.

* Physical maladies are always a sign of inner discontent. "Emotion" is energy in motion. If you stifle this energy, it will manifest in some other way.

* The thing you fear most in life has the potential to be your greatest teacher. But you do not learn by avoiding fear, you learn by moving into it.

* The only way out is through.

Namaste

APPENDIX: CANCER BLOG

My 1998 Cancer Experience

(Written as an online blog / journal 1998-1999)

2016 Note: I'm including this chapter in this book (essentially in its original form) because over the years, many other cancer patients have told me reading the notes of someone who survived chemotherapy and radiation actually helped them through their own cancer experience.

On January 9, 1998, I had a needle biopsy done on a suspicious lump in my neck. They did not like the look of the cells from that test, so on January 13 they removed the entire lymph node. By the end of that week they had a preliminary diagnosis of Hodgkin's lymphoma (a form of cancer of the lymph nodes). The final diagnosis was soon completed and the result was indeed Hodgkin's lymphoma (nodular sclerosing with syncytial variance, Stage III-2-A-S) and I started chemotherapy on February 6, 1998.

My first chemotherapy appointment involved a drug combination called ABVD. In the days following that treatment I never got nauseous to the point of vomiting. For the first few days I was only very tired and had an extremely low energy level. My taste buds were also affected, so eating was no longer fun. I found the blander the food, the better. Anything with a strong flavor or smell would almost make me nauseous. I had been taking several herbal medicines, but the taste and smell of them was no longer tolerable. During the second week following treatment, my energy level and appetite began to return, but I felt achy throughout my entire body, very similar to having the flu. As the days went by, I continued to feel better and better, to the point of almost feeling normal, just in time for the next chemo session.

The second chemo appointment on February 19 went much better than the first. They measured some of the readily palpable tumors, and they were already getting measurably smaller! (YEAH!!!) I took along a friend who's a hypnotherapist, and she used hypnosis with me before and during the chemo. This had the effect of making the appointment go much faster, and dramatically reduced the number of side effects. I still had very little nausea, had a much higher energy level, did not lose my appetite as much, and have had very little pain. The only major effect is that I lost all of my hair. Actually, it started falling out in handfuls, so I asked my wife to shave it all off. I bought another wig, this one with a "male" cut, and I wore it whenever I wanted to appear more normal. It also did a reasonable job of keeping my head warm during the remains of our Colorado winter.

On a scale of 1–10, with 10 being all the side effects they prepared me for, I would say after the first appointment I was a 6 or 7. After the last appointment I was about a 3. That is a LOT better, and with continued hypnosis, I expect the treatments to get better and better . . .

Update 3-22-98

My third appointment went well, too. I had my hypnosis in the morning for an afternoon appointment, and used "post-hypnotic suggestion" to get me through the chemo. That seemed to work as well as having the therapist there, as the side effects were about the same, or even slightly less. Now that I know a little about what to expect, that takes away some of the fear. I am still slightly nauseous at times, but nothing that a few minutes of time, or a nausea pill won't handle.

The worst side effect from this round was bad indigestion, which was combined with severe constipation and led to a really nasty case of hemorrhoids. My doctor gave me some meds for that, so those are now under control again. Can't you just hear my poor body screaming, "What is UP with all these DRUGS????" My medicine cabinet looks like a branch of the local pharmacy.

The tumors continue to shrink, and some of the nodes that my oncologist had been measuring have disappeared completely. HOORAY!

My fourth appointment was Thursday the 19th, and it was the best so far. My hypnotherapist was out of town, so I went to my massage therapist the morning of the appointment. She spent lots of time working on my energy levels, opening my "chakras" and doing hands-on "Reiki" therapy. This was combined with traditional massage, and so far, after three days, I have had minimal side effects, even less than the other appointments. I am becoming a firm believer in all these non-traditional adjuncts to the chemo.

My oncologist has decided that even though the chemotherapy is working well, she wants to add radiation therapy after the chemo is complete. It seems that my cancer is at a stage called "massive mediastinal involvement." That means that the space between my lungs, and around my heart, is completely filled with cancer. I saw the chest x-ray, and the tumors in that area involve almost a third of my chest area. Can you believe that you can have a cancer that fills that much space and still have NO symptoms from it? Because of that extensive involvement, the radiation seems to dramatically reduce the chance of relapse years down the road. I am not particularly fond of having more treatments, especially radiation, but have read the medical studies that back up the rationale for using it.

Update 4-14-98

Because of the future addition of radiation to the treatment plan, I have now had two chemotherapy treatments using a different drug combination called MOPP. This is a very old combination, but has less potential for lung or heart damage, so it is used when radiation will be needed later. The entire protocol is outlined in great detail online, if you are interested.

My side effects continue to be minimal, thanks to all your prayers, hypnotherapy, massage, Reiki, vitamins, etc. The MOPP combination seems to cause less nausea, although there is still some, but leaves me with an AWFUL taste in my mouth! It tastes like metallic ashes mixed with pepper. The taste is there all the time, and can only be masked by rinsing with baking soda water or lemon drops candy. The taste peaks about four days after the chemo, and hopefully will be gone in another few days. Due to this change, my taste buds now crave things that are strong and spicy! I have come 180 degrees on food preferences since the first couple of ABVD appointments, when bland was the order of the day. There are also some dietary restrictions with this combination. I can't have bananas or anything "aged," like wine, cheese, beer, pickles, alcohol, yogurt, etc.

Update 5-7-98

Eight down and four to go! (Two-thirds done with chemotherapy)

I had my eighth treatment today using MOPP. The day of chemo always goes well, as do the next couple of days, due to the heavy IV anti-nausea drugs they give just prior to the chemo meds. I expect to feel well again tomorrow, and then possibly feel a lowered energy level for a few days after that. The only significant new side effect after the last two appointments was a dramatic shift in my ability to sleep well. One of the "P's" in MOPP stands for Prednisone. That steroid has a history of causing hyperactivity and sleep disturbances, so no one was surprised to hear that I wasn't sleeping well. I usually awoke at somewhere between 2:30 and 4:30 A.M. and could not get back to sleep. The past week has not been so much that way. I actually slept in this morning until 7:30. I do have sleeping pills I can take, but prefer not to use them unless really needed.

I did have one interesting thing happen a couple of weeks ago. I came home from work feeling slightly nauseous. I took a relatively light anti-nausea pill that I had taken before, but for some reason it didn't do the trick. So about forty-five minutes later I took a Marinol capsule. (Pharmaceutical THC.) About thirty minutes after that, I was STONED out of my mind! The feeling most certainly brought back some of the memories I had during some college parties twenty to twenty-five years ago. There is definitely a certain "feel" to a cannabis high. The high was not very pleasant in that setting, as I was with my wife and children, and not at a big party where everyone else was stoned, so I just rested on the sofa and slept it off...

The tumors around my neck, collarbone, and in my armpits have shrunken so dramatically that they are essentially gone. I have an appointment for another CAT scan and chest x-ray in two weeks to verify that the internal tumors have responded as well as the ones easy to feel. I am confident that they have...

My oncologist even used the term "complete remission" today as their goal before radiation. I LIKED hearing those words as a real possibility!

Update 6-4-98

Today makes ten! (Only two to go?)

I go in today for chemo appointment number ten. If all goes according to plan I'll only have two left. I got the results of my recent CAT scan last week, and the results were good! As reported last month, the tumors are all shrinking or are gone completely. The nodes in my neck, collarbone area, armpits, and abdomen are completely gone. There is still a significant mass in my chest, about 2 inches in diameter and 4 inches long, but even that one has been reduced in size by over two-thirds. My oncologist says there is a good possibility that that mass may remain as harmless scar tissue for the rest of my life. They will continue to monitor that one, and if it continues to shrink during these last two months of treatment, they will add more chemotherapy before moving on to radiation. My spleen is still not normal in appearance, but considering it looked like Swiss cheese on the initial CAT scan, that doesn't surprise me. They don't seem particularly concerned about that either.

I have begun to regrow some hair, but it is very fine and light-colored. They will be returning me to the ABVD chemo today, so the hair growth may be short-lived. The initial combination of ABVD was what caused it to fall out in the first place.

I am sleeping much better lately and have seemingly adjusted to the Prednisone. A good night's sleep really helps a lot. I still can't really taste food in a "normal" way, but the bad metallic taste has lessened considerably. The other side effects continue to be relatively minor, but a recent twist has been a slight numbness in my fingertips. That hasn't caused a major problem for me yet, but if it worsens, it will definitely be a significant concern, since I'm a dentist. I have also had some mild bouts with nausea and depression, but I'm sure the two go hand in hand.

I'm just ready for this to all be over so I can get back to enjoying a "normal" life (including Alexus, of course). It seems that whenever they add a new drug to my schedule, it takes a couple of weeks or so for my body to adjust. Hopefully there will be no more additions to the list of side effects during this last six weeks of chemo.

Update 6-22-98
A little "detour" to the hospital.

On Sunday, June 14, I began to run a slight fever. My oncologist had warned me that any time I developed a fever of any sort, it was something to be concerned about. With the extremely low blood counts caused by chemo, even a mild infection can turn into a major event. I was also told that any fever of 101 degrees would result in immediate admission to the hospital for IV antibiotics. On Sunday night my fever was 100.5 degrees, so I took some Tylenol and went to bed. On Monday morning the 15th, I was still not feeling up to par, and had a new extremely sore spot on the side of my tongue. The spot was so sore it was affecting my speech, but with my typical "type A" personality, I went to work anyway. By mid-morning it was apparent that I wasn't going to make it through the normal workday, so I canceled the afternoon patients and went home at lunchtime for a nap. I slept for about two and a half hours and woke up with another fever. This time it was 101.5, so my wife called the oncologist, who told us to come to her office immediately.

As I had been warned I would be, I was admitted to the hospital in a matter of a few minutes. At that point, even though I was disappointed with the inconvenience of a hospital stay, I felt so bad I was ready for something to be done. They immediately drew blood for every conceivable test, took a chest x-ray, and began IV antibiotics.

I was diagnosed as "neutropenic" and anemic. Those terms mean I didn't have the normal amount of white OR red blood cells, so had no way to fight off any infection. A normal white blood count is 4800–10,000 and mine was 300. I was placed in a private room; visitors were required to wash their hands, and if they weren't 100 percent healthy, to wear a mask, before entering my room. I also had to wear a mask any time I left my room.

I was on IV antibiotics for three days. As my fever stabilized, my white blood counts began to rise, and I began to feel better. They then switched me to oral antibiotics. Even though my white counts were rising, my red blood counts were still falling from the depressed bone marrow caused by chemo.

On Friday I was given a transfusion of two units of whole blood, and released late afternoon. The blood tests never did turn up the cause for the infection, but during the previous week I'd had a few days of the "sniffles" and another bout with hemorrhoids. Either of those could have been the source of the infection, but since I was recovering, the original source was a moot point.

I spent a quiet weekend at home and took LOTS of naps. I'll be taking injections of Procrit three times per week for six weeks to stimulate my bone marrow. I also go in this Thursday, the 25th, for my eleventh chemo appt.

Update 7-23-98

The chemo is finally OVER!

I took my last IV chemotherapy treatment on July 2nd. That was followed by oral chemo meds for another week. And I must say, the last treatment was a rough one. I had to take something for nausea almost every day for a couple weeks. Hence the long time period between updates . . . But I'm finally feeling better! Hooray!!!! I haven't had to take anything for nausea for almost a week now. I'll have another two to three weeks to recover before I begin radiation therapy, but the side effects from that are supposed to be significantly less. My hands continue to be very weak and shaky and I think I'll probably have to go on complete disability from my dental practice very soon. My oncologist said the weakness will probably continue to get worse for a while before it starts to get better.

I go in on the 30th for another CAT scan to see if the cancer is completely gone. But regardless of what the CAT scan shows, they still want to do radiation "just to be sure." And since I never want to go through this again, I'll go along with anything that will reduce the chances of it coming back. I'll post the results of the scan as soon as I know them.

Since I am feeling so much better, I think Alexus will be out kicking up her heels again very soon :-).

Update 8-30-98
Radiation Therapy starts tomorrow . . .

The results of my CAT scan last month were very encouraging. All the cancer is gone except for a mass still remaining in my chest, and even that has been reduced in size by two-thirds. They say the mass is probably scar tissue and will likely never go away, but since they don't know that for certain they still want to do daily radiation therapy for three weeks. The best news from the scan is that my spleen has returned to normal as well. That means they won't need to irradiate below the diaphragm, which dramatically reduces the amount of nausea and other side effects. They say I will probably be very tired during the treatments, but it should be MUCH better than during chemotherapy. I'm certainly in favor of that!

The longest part of the radiation therapy was the preliminary workup. This appointment required that I lie flat on my back, with a pillow under my neck and shoulders, on a hard table, with my hands under my hips. While I was in this position they took x-rays from assorted and various angles to evaluate the exact areas they want to "zap." The only problem was that I had to lie in that position, completely motionless, for almost an hour and a half! I was about to go crazy by the time they finally allowed me to sit up! They assured me that the actual treatments would take only a few seconds each.

I continue to feel stronger every day, but still haven't been out on the town lately. My legs are still too weak to walk in heels, and my eyelashes have not yet grown back in. My toes and fingertips are still partially numb, so doing my makeup might also be a bit of a challenge.

I am now on partial disability, but will probably go on total disability during and/or after the radiation . . . so I doubt if I'll be able to make it to Atlanta for the SCC.

Update 10-31-98
ALL DONE with therapy!

My goodness was September a LONG month! They originally had me scheduled for fifteen radiation treatments (every day, five days a week, for three weeks). But due to the Labor Day holiday, and their decision to increase the number of treatments from fifteen to twenty-one, I had an appointment at 1:45 P.M. every weekday for the entire month of September!

The first week went along with few side effects, but I began to develop radiation burns on my skin during the second week and had to go on full disability from work. By the end of the original fifteen sessions, I was starting to look like an overcooked lobster. By the third week I could no longer tolerate wearing even a light T-shirt. Fortunately I discovered some silk shirts in my closet that I could wear after removing the tags in the back. Most of the burns were to my neck and shoulders, mostly on the back. The best description I can give is that it's like a VERY BAD sunburn, followed by another day in the sun, and another, and another.

The radiation also dried my mouth and burned my throat and esophagus so that swallowing was very difficult. I almost choked to death on a vitamin pill twice, so had to stop taking those for a while. The discomfort was bad enough that I had to take pain meds for the last couple weeks, and again had to resort to sleeping pills to get any rest at night. But that's ALL DONE now! I have almost healed from the radiation burns and go in for another CAT scan next Tuesday. Then my oncologist says she won't need to see me for three months. She's a wonderful person, but I must admit, I'm happy for the break.

As a result of the severe radiation burns and the continued weakness and loss of coordination in my hands, I've gone on complete medical disability and have, in fact, sold my dental practice. I've never been on disability or been unemployed in my entire adult life. This will take some getting used to!

The highlight of October was a MUCH-NEEDED vacation! After healing from the burns for a couple weeks, I felt well enough to go with my wife to Costa Rica for ten days. We had never been there before, and can't wait to get back. In fact, I'm thinking of taking a badly needed sabbatical from work and spending several months in the rain forest after the first of the year. What a high-energy place that was! I think it would be a great place to get in some serious healing, and to ponder the simple question, "What is the meaning of Life?"

Update 12-8-98
"Qualified Remission"

Those are just about the best words a cancer patient can hear! They came after my November CAT scan and chest x-rays. They are using the word "qualified" because of some remaining tissue in my chest. If you recall, from the very beginning the largest tumor mass was in the center of my chest, between my lungs and around my heart. Hodgkin's disease is known for leaving scar tissue behind even after all the cancer cells have been killed by chemo and/or radiation. Because of that remaining mass, they can't say I'm in complete remission until the mass has been monitored for a few months with additional x-rays. If it continues to shrink, or at least doesn't begin to grow again, they will then use the term "complete" remission. I'm not worried, and they don't seem at all concerned about it either.

In the meantime, I'm getting stronger every day, and have even been out as Alexus a few times. Keep checking my stories page for more details, because not only is she back . . . she's back with a vengeance! I have been broadening my femme horizons in ways I never dreamed possible before the cancer. This is partly because I sold my dental practice in early October and so have absolutely nobody to answer to except myself. This has given me the mental freedom to express en femme in a variety of new and wonderful ways. Stay tuned . . . and as they say, "You ain't seen nothing yet!"

Aesthetic Illusions is also up and running again, and I had a new, all-day client come to Denver from Kansas City last week. We had an absolute BLAST!

Update 2-4-99
COMPLETE REMISSION!!!!!

On Monday, February 1, 1999, I got just about the best news a cancer patient can get. I am in complete remission from my Hodgkin's disease. I had an appointment the previous Thursday to review my latest x-rays, but the radiologist's report was a bit confusing for both my oncologist and me. The report said it was a "normal" chest x-ray! We both thought the report was some sort of mistake, since my last CAT scan taken in November still showed a significant mass in my chest. So, to clear up the confusion, my oncologist wanted to meet with the radiologist and review the films with him in person. But after seeing the films with her own eyes, she was delighted to call me to say, "The films were normal!"

We had hoped the mass would continue to shrink, but to go from a "significant mass" to a "normal x-ray" in only three months was more than either of us had hoped for! It just goes to prove, there IS power in prayer!

I just want to say, once again, THANK YOU, EVERYONE, FOR YOUR PRAYERS!!!! They have been answered! :-)

I continue to get a little misty-eyed when I consider the love and support I have received from friends ALL over the world (most of whom I have never met in person)! I simply cannot put into words the love and gratitude I feel toward all of you . . .

Okay, now that the keyboard is moist from my tears of joy, on to additional fun news . . .

At the Thursday appointment prior to my great news, I "came out" to my oncologist, and indirectly to her staff. I felt it was time for her to know all about me, since I had placed my life in her hands almost a year ago. I also wanted her to know the "complete picture" in regards to my gender desires, as I have decided to go on full hormone replacement therapy and begin my transition. I wanted her blessings before moving ahead with this major step, to be sure there were no chances that the hormones could "stir up" anything this soon after chemo and radiation (my prescribing ob/gyn was also concerned about this).

My oncologist was not only supportive, she allowed her nurse to give me my estrogen injection. (I brought it along for the appointment, just in case . . .) Her entire staff was SO loving and supportive of my confession that I later brought back my pictures, and a dozen roses for them to share.

So once again, for those of you who have written with letters of prayer and support, and to those who have been praying for me in silence, I sincerely say "THANK YOU, THANK YOU, THANK YOU" . . . (even if I did not have the time or energy to answer you personally).

Acknowledgments

This is the first book I have ever written and I had no idea how difficult it would be or how long it would take. Without the help, guidance, and inspiration of a significant number of very important people in my life, this book would have never been written.

Thank you Debbie for unconditionally accepting me for who I am, here and now, and for never getting hung up on what might have been before.

Thank you Mom and Dad for teaching me the value of honesty, integrity, and above all, strength of character. I am who I am because of that strength. And that same strength allowed my older sister, Claudia, and my younger brother, Tracy, to quickly accept their new sister. Thank you both for that.

Thank you Nikki for your unconditional love and for taking me to that James Malinchak event. That event was pivotal in my realization that this book was actually possible. I am very proud of you!

Thank you Erika for being my stubborn little Taurus and keeping me on track with what it means to be a loving and supportive parent. You are simply amazing!

Thank you Cristina and Emily for believing in me at a time when I thought I might never be loved again. After my divorce and throughout my transition, you were my touchstones.

Thank you Shirlee Robinson of Leading Lady Photography in Aurora, Colorado. You artistry showed me just how beautiful I could be at a time when I really needed the inspiration and courage.

Many thanks to my writing coach and editor, Brooke Warner of Warner Coaching. Without her help and guidance, this book would have taken even longer to write and, in the end, would certainly have been much less polished and readable. I would also like to thank my editor, Krissa Lagos, and designer Tabitha Lahr, for creating a cover I am proud to have represent my book in the world. It takes a village to create a book, and I'm grateful to my whole team.

About the Author

Alexus Sheppard is a retired dentist with an undergraduate degree in Secondary Education. She began her transition from male to female after surviving stage 3 Hodgkin's Disease in 1998.

In 1996, prior to her transition, she began her online presence with a personal website, www.alexussheppard.com. This website became quite popular within the transgender community and quickly grew into a popular blog which documented both her pre-transition and post-transition life. That blog served as the inspiration and foundational material for this book.

She has been a guest lecturer, speaking on her transition and other LGBT issues, for numerous colleges and universities in both Colorado and California.

She now lives in Northern California with her wife Deborah.

www.ingramcontent.com/pod-product-compliance
Lightning Source LLC
Chambersburg PA
CBHW020610300426
44113CB00007B/589